Answering the Call

Answering the Call

Ethan L. Ketterer

DEDICATION

To every hero who answers the call.

To the **educators** who teach with heart,
the **administrators** who lead with vision,
the **counselors** who listen with compassion,
the **school safety officers** who protect with courage,
and the **teaching assistants and paraprofessionals** who hold
classrooms together with steady hands and unwavering
dedication.

You are the quiet strength in moments of crisis.
You are the voice of reassurance when a child feels unseen.
You are the steady presence when the day demands more than
expected.
You show up—not just because it's your job, but because it's
your *calling*.

You represent everything the KTURN brand stands for:
motivation, inspiration, encouragement, and empowerment
in action.

This book is dedicated to you—
the ones who lift students higher,
who carry burdens no one else knows about,
and who continue to give, serve, and stand… even when it costs
you something.

Your work is noble.
Your sacrifice is real.
Your presence is power.

Your presence is necessary.

This is your honor.
This is your recognition.

This is your moment.
This is your KTURN.

AUTHOR'S NOTE

There are moments in life that shape us, moments that test our strength, our purpose, and our calling. For me, one of those defining moments occurred on **September 19, 2018**—a day that began like any other in the In-School Suspension room, but ended with an incident that forever changed the way I viewed the work we do in schools.

The events that unfolded that day were not simply the result of conflict between students. They were the product of miscommunication, broken protocols, and a lack of information that allowed tension to grow unchecked. By the time everything reached my doorway, I found myself standing between a vulnerable student and a rapidly escalating situation. What followed was a violent attack—one that left me injured, shaken, and desperately calling out for help.

Yet even in that painful moment, I realized something profound:

There are countless men and women who stand in that gap every single day.

Educators. Administrators. Counselors. Teaching assistants. Paraprofessionals. School safety officers.
They show up—sometimes short-staffed, sometimes overlooked, sometimes carrying burdens no one else sees—because they are answering a call that is bigger than their job description.

This book is not about the attack itself.
It is about **the people who keep showing up after the attack**—
the ones who still choose to protect, to guide, to stand strong, even when the world has no idea what they face.

It is about the teaching assistants and paraprofessionals who hold schools together—not with authority, but with presence, patience, and heart. It is about the school safety officers who walk every hallway, the counselors who speak life into discouraged students, and the administrators who carry the weight of decisions that ripple across entire communities.

It is about **heroes who rarely receive the title.**

Writing this book was part of my healing.
But more importantly, it is part of my mission.

Through the KTURN brand, my heart has always been to **motivate, inspire, encourage, and empower**. This book continues that work by shining a light on those whose stories may never be told, but whose impact is felt in every classroom, every hallway, and every life they touch.

If you serve in a school in any capacity, know this:
You are seen.
You are valued.
You are vital.
And your calling matters.

Thank you for standing in the places where others cannot.
Thank you for choosing compassion even when the day challenges you.
Thank you for answering the call.

May this book honor your courage, affirm your purpose, and remind you that the work you do is nothing short of transformative. Your continued presence is requested.

— *Ethan L. Ketterer*

TABLE OF CONTENTS

INTRODUCTION

The Day Everything Changed

Schools are living, breathing communities—full of movement, emotion, tension, and triumph. Every day, thousands of adults step into their roles committed to shaping lives, protecting futures, and guiding students through challenges seen and unseen. Most days follow a familiar rhythm: quiet morning routines, crowded hallways, classroom chatter, lunchtime noise, end-of-day dismissal.

But every person who works in education knows there are days that defy the rhythm.
Days when routine dissolves into uncertainty.
Days that demand more strength than anyone expected.
Days that change you.

For me, that day was **September 19, 2018**.

It began like any other morning. I reported to the In-School Suspension room—a role I took seriously, not because it held prestige, but because it held responsibility. Students came to ISS carrying weight, emotion, frustration, or confusion. My job was to meet them where they were, provide structure, and make sure the room remained a safe, calm space.

On that particular morning, there was already a heaviness in the building. Something unspoken. Something unsettled. It was the residue of an incident from the day before—an incident involving two students whose stories had become tangled through rumors, partial truths, and miscommunication.

The previous day's conflict had never been properly sorted. No structured follow-up, no clear communication with families, and no unified understanding among staff. A student, upset and fearful, had contacted a parent before any school official could intervene or provide clarity. The emotions shared in that conversation—raw, unfiltered, and incomplete—spread faster than any official report could be made.

When communication breaks, safety loosens.
When clarity is missing, tension grows.
And when protocols fail, consequences follow.

All of that came to a head the next morning.

A Morning Filled With Signs

The young lady involved in the previous day's incident walked into the ISS room shortly after the day began. Her posture told the story before she spoke—shoulders tense, expression tight, eyes full of questions and frustration. She had been instructed to report to ISS, but she quickly realized that the other student from the conflict was *not* assigned to the room.

Confusion turned to disappointment.
Disappointment turned to anger.
And anger, when left unaddressed, becomes fuel.

I spoke with her calmly, reassuring her that I would reach out to her parent. I understood her frustration. I understood the feeling of not knowing. She deserved answers—not rumors, not guesses, not silence.

I contacted her father multiple times before finally reaching him. He listened intently, and although concerned, he assured me he would come to pick her up. But he had another daughter to retrieve from another school first. He told me he would be there as soon as he could.

In the meantime, emotions continued to simmer.

The young lady remained restless. She walked out of the ISS room repeatedly—not out of defiance, but out of distress. And as required, I followed her every time. She could not be unaccompanied in the hallway. Her safety was in my hands. I walked with her, talked with her, encouraged her, tried to ease her mind while also ensuring she remained supervised.

It was during one of those moments—another walk down the hallway—that everything changed.

The Corner That Changed Everything

There are moments in life you can never forget. Moments etched not only in memory but in muscle—your body remembers the shock, the tension, the fear long after your mind tries to let go.

As we rounded the corner that day, I saw them.

The other student from the alleged incident.
And three adults.
Standing together.
Staring directly at us.

The temperature in the hallway seemed to shift instantly. I felt the young lady beside me tense. Her breathing changed. Her pace changed. Her posture stiffened.

Before I could redirect her… she broke into a run.

Before I could call out… the group charged toward us.

Before I could secure the hallway… we were surrounded.

The hallway erupted into chaos within seconds. The student I was walking with became the target, and without hesitation, I placed myself between her and the danger. My training, my duty, my instinct—all aligned in that one decision.

Protect the student.

I shielded her with my body, but in doing so, I became the one attacked.
The blows came fast.

Punches.
Kicks.
Stomps.
Hands and feet striking with force and fury.

The noise of the struggle echoed against the walls—shouting, crying, the scuffling of shoes against tile. I reached for my walkie-talkie and called for help.

"I need assistance!"
Nothing.
"I need help—now!"

It felt like an eternity before anyone responded.

Pain radiated through my body. My balance shifted. My vision blurred. But the student behind me—frightened, shaking—remained my focus. I had answered the call to protect her, and I would not move until help arrived.

When additional staff finally reached us, the attack ended. But the impact—physically, emotionally, mentally—was only beginning.

More Than an Injury

Healing from physical wounds is one thing.

Healing from the knowledge that you were harmed while doing everything right…
that takes longer.

The days after the attack were filled with reflection, confusion, and disbelief. I questioned how communication had broken down so severely. I questioned how protocols had been overlooked. I questioned how safety could unravel so quickly.

But most of all, I thought about the countless educators, paraprofessionals, teaching assistants, school safety officers, counselors, and administrators who face similar risks and emotional burdens every single day.

I realized my story was not an isolated moment.
It was part of a larger truth:

Schools are kept standing by people who answer the call—even when it costs them something.

The people in our buildings are more than job titles.
They are protectors.
Guides.
Mentors.
Peacekeepers.
Advocates.
First responders in moments no one expects.

They show up.
They stay present.
They stand in the gap—even when the world does not see it.

A Journey of Purpose and Honor

This book is not about blame.
It is not about resentment.
It is about **recognition**.

Recognition for the unseen work.
Recognition for the everyday sacrifices.
Recognition for the courage required to protect children.
Recognition for those who continue to show up despite fear, frustration, or fatigue.

My hope is that as you read this book, you will walk with me through the moments before, during, and after that day. That you will see the humanity behind the headlines. That you will feel the heart behind the uniform, the badge, the ID tag, or the classroom key.

And most importantly:

My hope is that you will follow me on this journey as we explore how answering the call more than once is often required before we see the growth, the safety, the healing, and the success that our schools—and our communities—so desperately need.

We do not become stronger through a single moment.
We become stronger through the moments that test us repeatedly.
The moments that call us again
and again
and again.

This book is an invitation:
To honor those who serve.
To acknowledge their courage.
To elevate their stories.
To understand their weight.
And to celebrate their resilience.

This is the story of that day.
This is the story of its lessons.
This is the story of its heroes.

Welcome to **Answering the Call**.

CHAPTER 1
Heroes Walk These Halls

Every school morning begins long before the first bus pulls up. The heroes of the building — often unseen — arrive early, unlock doors, straighten desks, power up computers, lay out materials, respond to emails, and prepare themselves mentally for whatever the day may bring.

Some arrive before sunrise, driving through quiet streets while the rest of the world sleeps. Others walk into the building carrying the weight of their own personal lives — sick family members, financial pressures, emotional stresses — but somehow find the strength to set those concerns aside to serve the children entrusted to them.

By the time students enter the building, most staff have already been working for an hour or more.
And yet, few people ever see this part.
Few ever ask about it.
Few ever acknowledge it.

But **it matters**.

It matters because it shows the heart of those who serve.
It matters because it reveals a truth that many never stop to consider:
Schools work because people work.
Not for applause, not for cameras, not for recognition — but because they care.

This is why I say with full confidence:

Heroes walk these halls every single day.

The Quiet Heroes

In every school, you can find heroes in places most people never think to look.

You see them in the teacher who stays after school with a child who needs extra help.
You see them in the paraprofessional who walks a student through their frustration until their breathing calms.
You see them in the counselor who helps a child navigate emotions too heavy for their age.
You see them in the custodian who notices a student crying in the hallway and offers a quiet moment of reassurance.
You see them in the cafeteria worker who slips an extra fruit cup to a child she knows hasn't had breakfast.
You see them in the school safety officer who stands outside in the cold, making sure every student enters safely.

This is the side of education that doesn't make the headlines.
This is the side that rarely gets thanked.
This is the side that makes all the difference.

The Hum of the Hallway

If you stand in a school hallway long enough, you begin to notice the subtle shifts in energy.
The laughter of students who feel safe.
The footsteps of teachers moving quickly to address small issues before they grow.
The firm but gentle voice of a paraprofessional redirecting a

student headed down the wrong path.
The calm assurance of a safety officer monitoring the
environment, aware of every detail.

There is life in a school, a heartbeat that rises and falls with the
people inside it.
And each person adds something to the rhythm.

Some add structure.
Some add warmth.
Some add protection.
Some add encouragement.
Some add direction.

But together, they add stability.

Students feel it.
They depend on it.
They need it.

They may not always understand it, and they may not always say
it, but they know who is there for them. They know who they can
trust. They know who sees them.

Because presence speaks louder than words.

The Weight No One Sees

While the outside world often imagines schools filled only with
smiling children, colorful posters, and neatly arranged classrooms,
the reality is more complex.

Behind every lesson is a teacher managing academic expectations while trying to reach students who may be distracted by hunger, grief, fear, or trauma.

Behind every hallway duty is a paraprofessional balancing supervision with emotional support.

Behind every crisis response is a safety officer scanning the room, assessing risk, and stepping in even when the situation is unpredictable.

Behind every administrative decision is someone measuring the impact on hundreds of lives at once.

Most people will never see the tears educators hold back until after the dismissal bell.
They'll never see the nights staff go home feeling like they gave everything and still wonder if it was enough.
They'll never see the weight educators carry home — the stories they can't share, the concerns they can't shake, the students they worry about even in their sleep.

And still…
They show up.

This is not weakness.
This is dedication.
This is the calling.

Paraprofessionals & Teaching Assistants: The Foundation No One Talks About

If you really want to understand the strength of a school, pay close attention to the paraprofessionals and teaching assistants.

They are often the first to notice when a student's mood is off.
They are often the first to intervene when a situation begins to escalate.
They are often the ones students trust enough to share their struggles with.
They are often the bridge between students and the greater school team.

They walk hallways, supervise cafeterias, escort students, monitor behaviors, support instruction, assist special needs students, de-escalate conflicts, manage emotional breakdowns, and step in wherever they are needed.

Their work is not optional.
It is foundational.

And yet, they are often the ones the world forgets.

This book is committed to making sure that stops.

Your work matters.
Your presence matters.
Your sacrifices matter.

Why Courage Is the Culture of Education

To work in a school is to work in a constant cycle of unexpected moments — moments that test patience, compassion, and decision-making.

Educators do not simply teach lessons; they hold emotional space for the wounded.
Paraprofessionals do not simply supervise; they protect.
Safety officers do not simply monitor; they prepare for the unimaginable.
Counselors do not simply advise; they heal.

These roles require courage — not in rare, dramatic moments, but in everyday interactions.

Courage looks like stepping into an escalating situation without hesitation.
Courage looks like choosing patience when frustration rises.
Courage looks like returning day after day despite challenges.
Courage looks like believing in a child who has stopped believing in themselves.

Courage looks like **answering the call**, again and again.

Why This Chapter Matters

Before we walk deeper into the events that unfolded on September 19, 2018 — before we look at the communication breakdown, the protocol failures, and the violent attack that changed my life — it is important to ground this book in honor.

Honor for the people who make schools run.
Honor for the people who protect children.
Honor for the people who stand in the gap.
Honor for the people who answer the call — not once, but
repeatedly.

This chapter is your reminder that you are seen.
That your work is sacred.
That your presence is powerful.
That your heart is not invisible.
That your courage is not forgotten.

The chapters ahead will take you through difficult moments of
truth, but before we go there, this foundation must be set:

Heroes walk these halls.
And this book is for them.

***

Reflection Questions — Chapter 1: Heroes Walk These Halls

1. **Who in your school resembles the definition of a "quiet hero," and what makes their presence impactful?**
2. **Think about a time when you showed up for a student in a way no one else noticed. How did that moment shape your sense of purpose?**
3. **What are some of the invisible responsibilities you carry daily that others may overlook or underestimate?**
4. **Reflect on a moment when your presence alone helped calm a situation. What does this reveal about your influence?**

5. Which members of your school's staff do you believe deserve more recognition? How can you begin acknowledging them more intentionally?
6. How do you handle the emotional weight of your role when it becomes overwhelming? What strategies support your resilience?
7. Describe a moment that reminded you why you chose to work in a school. How does that moment continue to fuel you?
8. What does courage look like in your role on an ordinary day, not just in moments of crisis?
9. How can you contribute to creating a stronger culture of honor, support, and teamwork within your building?
10. Where do you feel your calling is leading you next — and what steps can you take to follow it with confidence?

CHAPTER 2
When Protocols Fail

Protocols are the backbone of a school. They are the anchor lines that prevent chaos, confusion, and crisis. Every school has them — policies for communication, discipline, supervision, parent contact, student movement, crisis escalation, and follow-up. These are not optional guidelines or suggestions; they are designed to protect students and to protect staff.

But protocols, no matter how well written, only work when they are followed.

When they are ignored…
when they are delayed…
when they are altered at the last minute…
when they are communicated inconsistently…

Safety weakens.
People get confused.
And students get hurt.

On the day before the incident that changed my life, that weakening had already begun.

The First Domino: 9/18/2018

The previous day's alleged incident involved two students whose relationship had already been tense. What should have been handled immediately, with clarity and structured follow-up, became tangled in miscommunication and silence.

The first student involved — frightened, emotional, uncertain — contacted a parent herself before any staff member could provide accurate information.

In that moment, one decision — one call made in distress — created a gap wide enough for misunderstanding to take root.

When protocols are followed:

- Staff contact parents.
- Administrators conduct investigations.
- Students receive emotional support.
- Facts are verified before conversations escalate.
- Information flows through appropriate channels.

But because this first step was skipped, the entire system became reactionary instead of proactive.

This was not the fault of the student.
This was not the fault of the parent.

It was the fault of a **system that did not move quickly enough**, leaving a young person to explain a situation she did not fully understand.

Her version of events was not malicious — it was emotional.
It was incomplete.
And it was enough to alarm a parent who wanted to protect their child.

By the next morning, the school was walking into a storm it didn't realize it had created.

The Silent Spread of Misinformation

Schools run on communication — formal and informal. When clear, communication builds trust and ensures safety. When unclear, it becomes a whisper network that spreads anxiety like wildfire.

By the morning of September 19:

- Some staff had pieces of the story.
- Some had only heard rumors.
- Some had no idea anything had happened at all.
- Parents were calling the office.
- Students were exchanging fragmented details.

In the places where truth should have been, uncertainty filled in the blanks.

Students sense tension instantly.
They carry emotions from home into school.
They feed off silence.

When children don't understand something, they fill the gaps with imagination — and imagination fueled by fear becomes a dangerous storyteller.

The tension in the air didn't feel like rumor.
It felt like a warning.

The Student's Arrival to ISS

When the student involved in the previous day's conflict entered the ISS room on the morning of 9/19, she walked in with the weight of everything she didn't know.

Her steps were brisk and uneven.
Her breathing was unsteady.
Her eyes darted around the room like she was searching for something that wasn't there.

Before she sat down, she asked the question that revealed everything:

"Is the other girl here?"

And when she realized the answer was **no**, her body stiffened.

Her anger was not random.
Her reaction was not surprising.

It was the natural response of someone who had been left alone with confusion for 24 hours.

Protocol calls for follow-up.
Protocol calls for explaining the plan.
Protocol calls for keeping involved students separated.
Protocol calls for communication with families.

None of that happened.

So in her eyes, the school's decision didn't feel procedural —
It felt personal.
It felt unfair.
It felt like betrayal.

And betrayal — whether real or perceived — is powerful fuel.

A Young Person Trying to Understand the Unfairness

One of the greatest challenges students face is interpreting adult decisions through their youthful lens. Adolescents are deeply sensitive to fairness, equity, and perception. When they believe an injustice has occurred, they don't see nuance — they see imbalance.

To her, the situation looked like:

- *She* was punished.
- *She* was isolated.
- *She* was assigned ISS.
- Meanwhile, the other student was walking freely.

She forced back tears and replaced them with frustration.
She folded her arms tightly across her chest, not in defiance, but to brace her heart.

Students often don't know how to ask for clarity.
They show their questions through their emotions.

And her emotions that day were asking:
"Why am I the only one here?"
"Why does it seem like I'm the only one in trouble?"
"Why didn't anyone explain what's going on?"

But children rarely say the questions out loud.
They show them.

And on this day, she showed them through pacing, leaving the room, and restless frustration.

The Repeated Exits — A Student in Distress

Students don't wander out of ISS repeatedly for no reason.
It's always a signal.

A signal of discomfort.
A signal of fear.
A signal of confusion.
A signal that processing isn't happening internally, so the body seeks movement externally.

Each time she exited the room, she moved faster.
Each time, her shoulders were more tense.
Each time, her voice was a little shakier — or a little louder.

She wasn't running away.
She was running *through* her emotions.

And because of the nature of my role, **I followed every time**.
Not to restrain her.
Not to "catch" her.
But because leaving her alone in that emotional state would have been unsafe.

Supervision is protection.
Presence is prevention.

Her safety depended on someone staying close.
And that someone was me.

The Teaching Assistant's Burden — Doing Everything You Can With What You Have

Walking behind her, I felt the weight that paraprofessionals and teaching assistants carry daily:

- We support students emotionally.
- We protect them physically.
- We monitor their movements.
- We interpret their behaviors.
- We de-escalate their frustrations.
- We fill in the gaps when systems fall short.

But while we do all that, we often do it **without the full information** we need.

Every time she left the ISS room, I followed with a heart that was steady but concerned. I didn't know all the details of the previous day's incident. I didn't know what had been communicated to the parents. I didn't know the other student was still in the building at that moment.

But I knew she needed supervision.
I knew she needed safety.
I knew she needed someone present.

And I did what so many paraprofessionals do every day:

I stepped in because the system didn't.

The Rising Tension in the Building

As we walked the hallway on one of her exits, I noticed something subtle — the kind of subtle shift only people who work in schools can feel.

The air changes before something happens.
The atmosphere tightens.
You sense something moving beneath the surface.
You can't see it, but you feel it.

The sounds of the hallway were slightly off.
Too quiet in some areas.
Too loud in others.
Students whispering in clusters.
Staff glancing toward certain corners.
Energy shifting.

These are signs that trained staff recognize instinctively.

And they're signs that go unnoticed when protocols have failed to keep the building emotionally secure.

How Small Failures Become Big Ones

The tragedy of that day was not caused by one big mistake.
It was caused by **a series of small ones**, piling onto one another until the weight became too heavy to ignore.

- **A delayed communication.**
- **An unanswered question.**
- **A frustrated student.**

- **A confused parent.**
- **An incomplete handoff.**
- **A lack of follow-up.**
- **Two students unwisely placed in proximity.**
- **A staff member left to manage a crisis without support.**

When each link in the chain weakens, the chain itself can no longer hold.

And on that day, the chain broke.

Walking Into Danger Without Knowing

As she walked ahead of me, her pace quickened.
She turned the corner sharply.
And in that split second, I felt something shift — the way you feel a gust of wind before a storm hits.

I stepped behind her, prepared to redirect her back toward the ISS room, hoping we could avoid more emotional escalation.

I didn't know what was around the corner.
But I knew something was there.

A school is filled with moments like these — moments when intuition is a better guide than policy.
Moments when you sense something before you see it.
Moments when instinct becomes your training.

And as soon as we turned that corner…

Everything that had been broken in the system
was about to break in real life.

The next moments would reveal the true cost of failed protocol.

And the cost was steep.

Reflection Questions — Chapter 2: When Protocols Fail

1. What examples in your school remind you that communication can make or break a situation?
2. How might clearer protocols have changed the outcome of the events described in this chapter?
3. Have you ever felt left to manage a situation without the information or support you needed? What emotions did that stir in you?
4. What strategies help you remain calm when you sense tension rising in your school environment?
5. Think of a student who reacted strongly to a situation they didn't fully understand. How did you support them, and what did you learn?
6. How can schools better reinforce fairness and communication so students don't feel blindsided by decisions?
7. What checkpoints should be in place after an incident to ensure clarity for both students and staff?
8. Where in your building do you see the greatest risk when protocols aren't followed consistently?
9. What role do paraprofessionals and teaching assistants play in navigating the gaps created by broken communication?

10. **How can you advocate for stronger, more effective protocols in your school community?**

Answering the Call

CHAPTER 3
A New Day, Old Tensions

No two school days are exactly the same. Some mornings begin with calm routines and familiar smiles. Others start with a hum in the air — the kind of hum that signals that something beneath the surface is moving, shifting, waiting to break.

September 19, 2018 was the latter.

Before I even placed my bag down in the In-School Suspension room, I knew the building was not the same as it had been the day before. The energy was heavier. The conversations shorter. The pacing of footsteps more intentional.

A building tells a story before anyone speaks.
And that morning, the story was unsettling.

Reading the Room Without Words

Teachers stood in their doorways, greeting students with smiles, but their eyes revealed something else — concern.
Paraprofessionals walked the hallways with slightly more intensity than usual — scanning, listening, anticipating.
Administrators moved with a firmness in their stride, as if they were trying to get ahead of something they already felt behind on.

The front office phone rang repeatedly.
Students whispered in pockets.

A few kept glancing down the hall, checking who might appear around the corner.

School buildings have atmospheres.
That day, ours was thick with uncertainty.

As staff, we learn to read cues that most people would miss. A slight shift in noise level. A change in tone during morning announcements. A hush falling over students who are normally loud. These cues become indicators — early warnings that trouble is walking around with its head down, waiting for a moment to stand up.

I sensed it.
And deep down, I hoped I was wrong.

The ISS Room Was Supposed to Be a Refuge — But Not That Day

The ISS room often serves as a safe place — not a punishment, but a structured environment where students can pause, reset, and regroup. On most days, I can help de-escalate students simply through presence, conversation, or a calm tone.

But on September 19, the ISS room felt different before the student even arrived. It felt like a place carrying too much from the day before — carrying unanswered questions, unresolved emotions, and unmet expectations.

When she walked in, the atmosphere shifted again.

Her face said everything her words did not.

She was tense, tired, confused, and frustrated all at once.
Her emotions were layered, resting beneath the surface like
stacked plates — fragile and ready to break if anything pressed
too hard.

She didn't sit down immediately.
Instead, she stood in the doorway, glancing around as if the room
itself would tell her whether today would be better than yesterday.

Her Silence Told the Story

Her body language was shouting long before her voice did.

She sat down, stood up, sat again, then stood once more.
Her leg bounced rapidly.
Her breathing was too fast.
Her fingers tapped the desk in inconsistent rhythms.

Students express stress differently, but in all my years of working
with young people, I have learned something important:

**When a student is overwhelmed, their body speaks before
their voice ever does.**

She didn't need to yell for me to know something was wrong.
She didn't need to complain for me to realize she was hurting.
She didn't need to misbehave for me to see that the system had
failed her.

All she said was:

"Is the other girl here?"

And when I answered honestly — "No" — her reaction was immediate.

Her shoulders tightened.
Her eyes narrowed.
Her eyebrows pulled together in confusion and disbelief.
Her breath caught in her throat.

Not anger.
Not resentment.
Not even fear.

But **betrayal**.

To her, the situation was suddenly imbalanced.
She had followed instructions.
She had come where she was told.
She had accepted the consequence — even if she didn't understand it.

Meanwhile, the other student involved in the incident appeared to be going about her day normally.

Students don't always articulate their sense of justice.
They *feel* it.

And that feeling can be powerful enough to shake an entire building.

The Questions She Didn't Know How to Ask

In that moment, I could see unspoken questions forming behind her eyes:

"Why am I being separated?"
"Why didn't anyone call home last night?"
"Why wasn't I checked on before I left yesterday?"
"Why am I the only one here?"
"Do they think I'm the problem?"
"Does anyone even care how scared I was?"

Children may not know how to phrase these questions, but they know how to live them.

And she was living them loudly.

Her pacing increased.
Her restlessness grew.
Her breaths became shallower.

Her silence was not calm — it was chaos.

When a Child Doesn't Know What to Do, They Move

She stood abruptly.

"I gotta walk," she said, voice trembling.

"Let's go," I replied gently. "I'm with you."

And so we walked.

Walking wasn't defiance.
It was survival.
It was her body's way of preventing breakdown.
It was her attempt to process what she couldn't understand.

As we moved through the hallways, her steps were inconsistent — fast, slow, fast again.
Her hands tugged nervously at her sleeves.
She glanced behind her repeatedly as if something unseen was following her.

She was not running away.
She was running *through* her confusion, fear, and frustration.

This is where paraprofessionals become more than staff — we become anchors.

She needed someone to tether her to safety, even if safety felt distant.

I followed her because supervision wasn't about compliance — it was about **presence**.

And on that day, presence was all we had.

The Sound of a Building Holding Its Breath

As we walked, I couldn't shake the feeling that we weren't alone in our tension.

In the hallway:

- A normally playful student stood still, watching her closely.
- A teacher lowered her voice mid-sentence and glanced toward us.
- A group of students paused their conversation as we passed.
- A safety officer turned slightly, observing the energy.

It felt like the building was holding its breath — waiting, watching, anticipating.

Tension like that doesn't come from one person.
It comes from something larger — a collective awareness that the day is not on stable ground.

And although I didn't yet know what we were walking into, I understood instinctively:

We were nearing something.
Something big.
Something none of us had been prepared for.

Her Father's Voice — Understanding, But Too Late

When I finally reached her father, he sounded calm but distressed.

"Mr. K… she called me yesterday. She was crying. I didn't know what was happening. I still don't know what's happening."

I apologized — not out of obligation, but because the failure was real.

He exhaled heavily.
"I'll come get her. I just need to get my other daughter first. I'm on my way."

I told her gently, "Your dad is coming. He's on his way."

She nodded, but relief did not soften her expression.

In her mind, the damage had already been done.

Children don't only react to what is happening —
they react to what *hasn't* happened.

And nothing had been done to bridge her understanding.

Walking With Her Was Walking With a Question

We resumed walking.

But this time, her movements were more frantic.

She turned corners sharply.
Her arms pumped harder as she walked.

She whispered to herself under her breath:

"This isn't fair…
I didn't do anything…
Why didn't they tell me…
Why is she not in trouble…
I'm so tired of this…"

She wasn't directing this at me.
She was speaking into her own pain.

And I stayed beside her, step for step, because this is what
support staff do — we walk into emotional storms with our
students even when we don't have umbrellas.

A Moment That Should Have Been Prevented

We had walked this hallway many times that morning, but this
time felt different.

She was moving faster.
I felt pressure rising in the air as if the atmosphere itself were
warning us.

She rounded a corner quickly — too quickly for me to call her
back.

And that's when everything slowed.

Because running right towards us, stood the other student involved in the prior day's incident…

and three adults.

Their presence alone shifted the hallway into a volatile space.
Their expressions were stern, serious, and focused.

Her body froze for half a second.
Her breath caught in her chest.

She continued walking.

Not away.
Not sideways.

Straight toward them.

Right into the collision course created by a system that failed to protect her.

And I followed — because I had to.
Because that was my responsibility.
Because supervision isn't optional when a child is in distress.
Because she needed me.

In that moment, we weren't just walking hallways.

We were walking into a situation made dangerous by silence.
A situation that could have been prevented.
A situation where protocols didn't just fail —
they disappeared.

And I knew as I the punches and kicks began to land:

The day had just changed.

Reflection Questions — Chapter 3: A New Day, Old Tensions

1. What signs of emotional distress do you see in students that often go unnoticed by others?
2. How does incomplete communication contribute to escalations or misunderstandings in your school?
3. Describe a time when a student's body language told you more than their words did. What did you learn from that moment?
4. How might early intervention after an incident change the direction of a child's next day?
5. Have you ever walked into a situation sensing danger before anything happened? What prepared you to recognize it?
6. How can administrators better support paraprofessionals and TAs who often become the "front line" in student emotional crises?
7. What systems could be put in place in your building to ensure students never feel as isolated as the young lady in this chapter?
8. How does fairness — or the perception of fairness — influence student behavior and trust?
9. What strategies help you stay calm when a student begins to spiral emotionally?
10. What role does "presence" play in safety, and how can school teams strengthen this habit?

CHAPTER 4
Walking the Hallway

Schools are living organisms. They breathe. They shift. They respond to the people inside them. And on some days, the building feels like it knows something before anyone else does.

September 19, 2018 was one of those days.

The moment we stepped into the hallway, it felt like stepping into a space where the air was too full yet eerily empty — a contradiction that only educators know how to recognize. A hallway can be loud with movement and still silent with tension. And that morning, tension was the loudest thing in the building.

I've walked these hallways hundreds of times.
But never like this.

The Hallway Had a Pulse

On an average day, the hallway hums with predictable energy:

- chatter from students
- quick footsteps of teachers between classes
- the distant ring of a classroom phone
- laughter bouncing off lockers
- the steady rhythm of routine life

But on this morning, the rhythm was disrupted.

Not broken — disrupted.

It was like the building was pulsing with something beneath the surface, as though everyone was waiting for a moment they couldn't quite name. Even students seemed to sense it. Children are perceptive; they notice emotional shifts long before adults acknowledge them.

I saw it in their eyes — curiosity layered with unease.
Not fear, but something close to it.
The kind of uncertainty that makes even the confident step lightly.

And the student walking in front of me mirrored that same energy.

Her Emotions Were a Storm She Couldn't Outwalk

Her pace was uneven — fast, then slow, then fast again.
Her posture was tight.
Her breathing came in quick, shallow bursts.

This wasn't restlessness.
This was distress.

She wasn't trying to get out of ISS — she was trying to get out of an emotional corner that the adults in the building had placed her in unintentionally.

Every step she took communicated pain.

I watched her hands open and close repeatedly, a subconscious attempt to release tension she didn't know how to name. Her legs moved with purpose, but her face carried confusion. Her eyes were alert, scanning corners, scanning doors, scanning shadows — not because she expected danger, but because she feared unexpected confrontation.

Children don't always want answers —
but they always want clarity.

She had none.
Not from yesterday.
Not from this morning.
Not from anyone who should have intervened earlier.

So she walked.
Because walking gave her a momentary illusion of control.

My Role: Keeping Her Grounded When She Felt Untethered

In situations like this, the job of a paraprofessional becomes more than supervision. It becomes grounding — emotional, physical, psychological grounding. You stay close because your presence is a protective barrier. You stay alert because the student is fragile. You stay calm because they cannot.

I walked behind her not out of obligation, but out of instinct.

An instinct built from years of working with students who carry more than their age should allow.
An instinct shaped by training and experience.
An instinct that tells you:

"If you step back now, she'll feel abandoned. If you stay close, she'll feel supported."

My steps matched hers.
Not too close.
Not too far.
Just enough to let her know I was there.

This was not about discipline.
This was about dignity.

She needed someone who wasn't judging her.
Someone who wasn't ignoring her.
Someone who wasn't minimizing her fears.
Someone who understood that her behavior was a symptom, not a problem.

So I stayed with her every second.

The Hallway Was Trying to Warn Us

Every school has moments where the emotional temperature can be felt before it's understood. And as we moved further down the hallway, the temperature dropped.

A teacher paused mid-sentence as we passed by.
A counselor looked in our direction longer than usual.
A safety officer tilted his head slightly, reading the situation with seasoned eyes.
Two students exchanged looks, whispering something quickly before turning away.

None of these actions were loud.
None were dramatic.
But together, they spelled something unsettling:

The building felt the storm before it arrived.

Educators develop a sixth sense — a quiet internal alarm that rings when something isn't right. Mine was ringing now.

Not urgently.
Not panic-level.
But enough to make me more aware of every sound, every movement, every shift in her behavior.

She Walked Faster — And With Each Step, Her Fear Spoke Louder

Her movements were no longer just restless — they were urgent.

"This isn't fair," she muttered.
"I don't understand why I'm in trouble."
"They didn't tell me anything."
"She gets to walk around? But I'm stuck in ISS?"

Her words tumbled out like small eruptions of emotional pressure.

I responded calmly:

"I hear you."
"I'm walking with you."
"I don't want you to get yourself in trouble."
"You're not alone."

But validation cannot undo miscommunication.
It can only lighten it.

And the miscommunication of the previous day sat on her
shoulders like a boulder she had been forced to carry by herself.

If she had been given clarity, support, or even a conversation, we
might not be walking these halls at all.

But we were.
And the weight was growing.

Every Footstep Echoed Tension

The hallway seemed to stretch longer the deeper we walked.

Lights buzzed overhead.
Sneakers squeaked faintly against the floor.
The building hummed with low-grade tension.

She sped up.
I matched her pace.

At one point, she turned her head halfway toward me as if
wanting to say something but swallowing the words instead. That
swallowed emotion created another layer of tension — one that
educators know well.

Students often speak their loudest truths through silence.

And her silence was screaming.

The Call From Her Father Should Have Brought Relief — But It Didn't

When I finally reached her father earlier, I could hear both concern and frustration in his voice.

"I'm coming to get to her," he said. "It's going to take me a little bit to get there because I have to pick my other daughter up from her school. I didn't know what was going on."

He wasn't angry — he was concerned.
He wasn't dismissive — he was present.

I assured him:

"I'm with her. I won't leave her alone. Come as soon as you can."

She overheard my end of the conversation.
Her shoulders lowered slightly.
But it wasn't relief — it was exhaustion.

The kind of exhaustion that comes from waiting too long to be understood.

Her father's promise to pick her up helped, but it didn't erase what she'd been sitting with all morning. Relief can only take hold when the storm has passed — not while you're standing in the middle of its winds.

And we were still very much in the wind.

Turning the Corner — and Stepping Into the Moment Everything Changed

She began walking faster — faster than any of the earlier laps.
I felt her urgency.
Something in her was pulling her forward, like she sensed
something ahead of us.

We approached the corner of a quieter hallway — one that always
felt too still during the school day.

She turned the corner sharply.

I followed immediately.

And then everything slowed.

Everything.

Because in that hallway —
standing in a cluster just far enough away to be concerning and
just close enough to be dangerous —
was the other student.

And she wasn't alone.

Three adults stood with her.
Their posture stiff.
Their expressions tight.
Their presence heavy.

The hallway thickened around us like air before a lightning strike.

The student in front of me froze.

Her breath caught.
Her hands tightened.
Her body leaned forward.

She whispered one word under her breath —
a word filled with shock, panic, recognition, and fear all at once:

"No..."

She continued walking.

Not running.
Not retreating.
Walking.
Straight toward the confrontation she didn't want but couldn't avoid.
Straight into the storm she had been carrying since yesterday.

And instinct overtook me.

I ran after her.

Because in that moment, I wasn't just an ISS teaching assistant..

I was her shield.

I was her barrier.

I was the person standing between a child's panic and a dangerous situation that had been created by adult silence.

———————————

A Hallway of Emotions Ready to Break

As she continued walking, everything happened at once:

- The adults stepped forward.
- The other student ran towards us.
- Voices rose.
- Emotions surged.
- The air felt electric.
- The hallway filled with movement from multiple directions.

I reached for her, not to restrain her but to protect her — because that's what the moment required.

My only thought:

**"Protect the child.
Protect her at all costs."**

I stepped beside her.
Then in front of her.
Then hovered over her.

And that was the moment —
the exact moment —
when the day changed.

The moment the storm finally broke open.

Reflection Questions — Chapter 4

1. What cues—spoken or unspoken—tell you when a student is emotionally overwhelmed?
   How do you usually respond?
2. How does isolation or lack of communication impact student behavior the next day?
3. Think of a time when your instincts told you something wasn't right before the situation escalated.
   What signs did you notice?
4. What role does physical movement play in helping students process emotional stress?
5. How can school staff collectively improve hallway safety and emotional awareness?
6. Have you ever been the only adult present during a rising conflict?
   How did you navigate the moment?
7. In what ways can schools improve communication with students immediately after an incident to prevent emotional spiraling?
8. What responsibilities do paraprofessionals carry that often go unseen or unsupported?
9. Describe a moment when you stepped into a situation instinctively.
   How did that instinct protect someone?
10. What systems or protocols could prevent students from walking into emotionally dangerous situations like the one described?

CHAPTER 5
The Attack — "I Need Help!"

It's strange how quickly a normal day can split into before and after.
One hallway.
One moment.
One split second where instinct and danger collide.

I stepped in front of the student not because I had planned to —
I stepped in front of her because something in me **knew** that if I
didn't, the situation would ignite in a way that could not be
undone.

Educators don't always have time to think.
Sometimes all we have is instinct.
And instinct is what placed me exactly where the danger would
land.

But I didn't know that yet.

All I saw was a child in distress and a hallway ready to erupt.

The Collision Point

She ran toward them — not out of rage, but out of desperation.

"NO! Why is she here?!" she screamed, her voice trembling.

Her legs carried her faster than her reasoning.
Her emotions sprinted ahead of her understanding.

I moved quickly, cutting the distance between us, placing myself
between her and the cluster of adults.

My arms stretched out in a protective stance.

"Back up," I said firmly. "Everybody take a step back—"

But no one stepped back.

Instead, everything stepped *forward*.

Emotions.
Voices.
Bodies.
Miscommunication.
Fear.
Misinterpretation.
Assumptions.

All of it crashed together at once.

A perfect storm created by the silence and mistakes of the day
before.

And I was standing dead center.

The First Strike — The World Tilts

I turned my head slightly to check on the girl behind me.

The Attack — "I Need Help!"

That half-second — that tiny sliver of divided attention — cost
me more than I could have imagined.

A fist connected with the side of my face.
Fast.
Hard.
Unrelenting.

My head jerked sharply.
A bright flash shot across my vision.
A buzzing sound filled my ears.

Before I could process the first blow, a second came —
then a third —
each one landing with precise violence.

Someone shouted.
Someone else gasped.
A student screamed.

But all of that felt far away, like echoes in a tunnel.

I stumbled but didn't fall.
Not yet.

My hands instinctively came up, not to fight, but to shield.

Another blow slammed into my temple.
My knees buckled, and my legs fought to hold me up.

I was losing the fight.

Hitting the Ground — And Becoming a Target

The ground rushed up without mercy.

I didn't fall gracefully.
I collapsed hard —
shoulder first, then ribs, then face.

Pain shot through my body like electricity.
My breath escaped in a violent exhale.

Before I could gather myself, a foot struck my side.
Then another.
And another.

Sharp.
Heavy.
Violent.

My ribs screamed.
My body curled involuntarily.
My mind reached for orientation but couldn't find it.

My left arm was kicked backward.
My right shoulder burned intensely.
A stomp landed on my back so hard I felt the shock in my jaw.

Voices blurred:

"Stop!"
"Get off of him!"
"Help him!"
"What are you doing?!"

"No! No!"
"Call someone!"

But the blows kept coming.

Pain Has A Sound

People who have never been assaulted don't realize that pain has
a sound.
It echoes differently.
It rings inside the skull.
It vibrates through the spine.
It makes time slow even as chaos speeds up.

My ears rang with a piercing whine.
My heartbeat thudded in my throat.
My vision pulsed in and out.

Everything felt both distant and overwhelming.

I tried to lift my head, but a foot pressed me back down.
I tried to cover my ribs, but a kick knocked my arm away.
I tried to breathe, but every inhale felt like fire.

Somewhere nearby, the student I was protecting screamed—

"STOP! LEAVE HIM ALONE!!!
PLEASE STOP! PLEASE!"

Her voice shattered something inside me.

This wasn't just an assault.
This was a trauma unfolding in front of a child already drowning
in confusion.

I had to protect her.
Even from the ground.
Even through pain.
Even while being beaten.

My body moved on instinct.
I twisted just enough to shield her with the only thing I had left
—

my own body.

The Walkie-Talkie — My Only Lifeline

With every ounce of strength I could gather, I reached for my
walkie-talkie.

My hand trembled violently.
My vision blurred.
My finger hovered over the button.

The first attempt failed —
my thumb slipped.
The second attempt barely made contact.

But the third attempt—

That one connected.

With breath ripping through my chest, I shouted:

"I NEED HELP!"

No response.

I shouted again, louder, pushing past the shock:

"I NEED HELP IN THE HALLWAY — NOW!"

My voice cracked.
The words tore out of me raw and desperate.

The attacks didn't stop.
But I couldn't stop either.

I pressed the radio again — my hands shaking uncontrollably.

"HELP! I NEED HELP RIGHT NOW!"

Those words became more than a call for backup.
They became a plea for survival.

They echoed off the walls.
They vibrated through the floor.
They carried down the hallway like an alarm bell.

And the building heard them.

Chaos Responds to Chaos

Suddenly, the sound of footsteps flooded the hallway.
Fast.
Hard.
Urgent.

Doors burst open.
Staff shouted orders.
People ran from every direction.

"Get off him!"
"Move back!"
"Stop right now!"
"Call security!"
"Call 911!"
"He's hurt — he's hurt!"

Hands grabbed arms.
Bodies were pulled apart.
People intervened.
Voices collided.

The assault began to break apart, but its damage did not.

Even as the blows stopped, the pain didn't.
My shoulder throbbed uncontrollably.
My ribs felt like they were on fire.
My head pounded with an ache that felt deeper than bone.

I was conscious — but disoriented.
Awake — but overwhelmed.
Present — but drifting.

Someone put a hand on my back.

"Don't move, Mr. K. Stay still."
"You're going to be okay."
"Help is on the way."

But I wasn't thinking about myself.

I turned my head, searching through blurred vision for the
student.

Finding Her — The Hardest Part Of the Moment

She was pressed against the wall, her hands covering her mouth, sobbing hysterically.

Her legs trembled so badly she could barely stand.
Her chest heaved with silent cries.
Her eyes were locked on me — wide, terrified, disbelieving.

In her mind, everything had collapsed.

Her safety.
Her trust.
Her understanding.
Her sense of control.
Her belief that adults always protect her.

She had watched the entire assault.
Every punch.
Every kick.
Every stomp.
She saw it all.

I lifted my hand slowly toward her — a small gesture, but everything I had in me.

"You're... safe..." I whispered.
"Don't... cry..."
"You... didn't... do anything wrong..."

She cried harder.

And that moment pierced me deeper than any physical blow.

Because no child —
no matter their role in a conflict —
no matter their circumstances —
no matter their mistakes —
should ever witness an adult being violently attacked while trying
to protect them.

But she had.

And it changed something in both of us.

The Body Keeps Score

Pain is not a single sensation — it is layers.

As I lay there, the layers stacked on top of each other:

- the throbbing in my head
- the stabbing in my ribs
- the burning in my shoulder
- the sharp ache in my arm
- the shockwave in my spine
- the ringing in my ears
- the swelling in my cheek
- the pounding of my pulse
- the tightening of my muscles in instinctive defense

I tried to push myself up.

My body refused.

A staff member pressed my shoulder gently but firmly.

"Don't move. You're hurt."

Another kneeled next to me.

"Breathe. Stay with us. Don't close your eyes."

But the truth was, my eyes *wanted* to close.
Not to sleep — but to escape.

My mind replayed every second of the assault in a loop —
the fists
the kicks
the screaming
the walkie-talkie
the voices
the pain

Trauma doesn't wait until later.
It imprints instantly.

And I felt it imprinting as I lay there.

Emergency Care Arrives

The nurse arrived first, sliding next to me with calm urgency.

"What hurts the most?" she asked.

I couldn't answer.
Not because I didn't know —
but because *everything* hurt.

She recognized that.
Her eyes softened.

"Okay. Don't talk. Just breathe."

Another staff member whispered:

"They're calling EMS."

I nodded faintly — then winced at the pain that shot through my neck.

The hallway was still buzzing with voices, but I only focused on one:

The trembling cry of the girl I had tried to protect.

It cut through every sound.

And it reminded me why I had stepped forward in the first place.

The Emotional Reality Sets In

As the adrenaline faded, a deeper realization formed:

This wasn't just a physical assault.
It was a failure.
A breakdown.
A preventable tragedy.

This moment was the result of:

- ignored protocols

- incomplete communication
- delayed follow-up
- unaddressed emotional needs
- assumptions
- fear
- misunderstanding
- and responsibility placed on the wrong shoulders

I didn't think of blame.
I didn't think of retaliation.
I didn't think of anger.

I thought of the system.

And how broken it had been that day.

Broken enough to leave a child unsupported.
Broken enough to create confusion.
Broken enough to allow two emotionally fueled students to collide.
Broken enough for violence to erupt.
Broken enough to leave me on the floor in pain.

And broken enough to traumatize a student who didn't deserve any of it.

The Hardest Truth: I Would Still Do It Again

Even through the pain, through the confusion, through the shock —

I knew one thing with absolute certainty:

If I had to make the same choice again,
if I had to step forward,
if I had to shield that student,
if I had to stand in the gap—

I would.

Because that's what answering the call looks like.

It looks like stepping forward when danger rises.
It looks like protecting children even when the cost is high.
It looks like standing in the space where fear and responsibility
meet.

And that day, I answered the call at full volume.

Even when the call answered back with violence.

Reflection Questions — Chapter 5

1. What emotions rose in you as you read this chapter
   — and why?
2. How do you think trauma impacts staff and students
   differently during and after a violent incident?
3. Have you ever been in a situation where your instinct
   took over faster than your reasoning? What guided
   you?
4. What systems should be in place to protect staff from
   having to step into danger alone?
5. What role did miscommunication play in the events
   that led to this moment?
6. How can schools better prepare staff to respond to
   crisis without sacrificing their own safety?

7. What support would you need after experiencing or witnessing a traumatic event like this?
8. How can administrators rebuild trust with staff and students after a violent incident occurs?
9. What does "answering the call" mean to you personally after reading this chapter?
10. In what ways can this story bring greater awareness to the hidden sacrifices school staff make?

CHAPTER 6
The Aftermath

When the last kick landed, the world didn't immediately snap back into place.
Trauma doesn't release you that quickly.
It lets go in pieces — slowly, painfully, unpredictably.

As I lay on the floor, surrounded by voices and hands trying to help me, time felt broken.
Some moments stretched out like slow-motion.
Others blinked past faster than I could register.

What I knew for certain was this:

The moment I hit the ground was the moment my life changed.
Not just physically —
but emotionally, mentally, spiritually.

The attack was over,
but its aftermath was just beginning.

The Hallway of Shock

People were everywhere.

Teachers.
Safety officers.
Paraprofessionals.

Administrators.
Students peeking from classroom doors.

The hallway that had been silent minutes ago was now filled with layered noise — overlapping voices, urgent commands, frantic questions.

"Give him space!"
"Get her back in the room!"
"Call EMS!"
"Stop recording!"
"Make room!"
"He's hurt!"
"He's not getting up!"

Someone knelt beside me.

"Mr. K, can you hear me?"

I tried to answer, but my mouth felt heavy and my head throbbed so violently that words came out slow and cracked.

"Yes…" I whispered, though I wasn't sure if it was audible or imagined.

My ribs hurt with every breath.
My shoulder felt like it had been torn from its socket.
My back screamed when I shifted even an inch.
And my head — my head pulsed like a drum being struck internally.

Shock is a strange thing — part numbness, part pain, part disbelief.
It wraps around the mind like fog, muffling logic and amplifying fear.

For a moment, I wondered if I had passed out.
For a moment, I wondered if I would again.

The Student's Cry — A Sound That Cut Through Everything

Her voice pierced through the chaos.

"Mr. K!
MR. K!!!
Are you okay?!
I'm sorry!
I'm so sorry!"

She was shaking so hard she could barely stand.
Someone guided her back toward the ISS room, but she fought it.

"I don't want to leave him!
Please!
He didn't do anything wrong!"

Hearing her cry was worse than being hit.

This was a child who had already been overwhelmed,
unprotected, unheard —
and now she had watched the only adult who stood with her get
violently attacked right in front of her eyes.

The trauma that moment etched into her spirit would last years.

No child should ever carry a memory like that.

And no staff member should ever be left to face danger alone.

The Nurse Arrives — The First Layer of Care

The school nurse arrived quickly and knelt beside me, her voice calm but urgent.

"Don't move, Mr. K. Stay right where you are."

She checked my pulse.
She checked my breathing.
She checked the swelling on the side of my head.

Her next words told me everything I needed to know:

"We need EMS. Now."

She said it quietly, but her tone was unmistakable.
It wasn't precaution.
It wasn't routine.
It was necessity.

I tried to lift my head and instantly regretted it.
A wave of pain shot through my neck and shoulder.
Black spots danced across my vision.

"Lie back," she said firmly. "You're hurt worse than you realize."

I wasn't sure what hurt more —
my body,
or knowing that a moment meant for protection had become a moment of pain.

The Adults Who Witnessed It — Their Faces Said Everything

As I lay there, I caught glimpses of staff members' faces:

Shock.
Fear.
Anger.
Sadness.
Guilt.
Helplessness.

Some of them had tears in their eyes.
Some were whispering prayers under their breath.
Some stood frozen, unsure how to process what they just saw.

In that hallway, for those minutes, everyone felt the weight of
failure —
failure of communication,
failure of protocol,
failure of timing,
failure of a system that left one staff member alone with a student
in distress.

And yet, in their eyes, I also saw something else:

Gratitude.

Because even in the chaos, they knew why I stepped forward.
They knew what I had been trying to prevent.
They knew the attack was not born from malice but from a
breakdown that should never have occurred.

They knew I answered the call.

And they knew the call had answered back cruelly.

EMS Arrives — And the Reality Sets In

The sound of distant sirens entered the building's atmosphere.

Moments later, EMS personnel appeared, kneeling beside me with urgency and precision.

"Sir, don't move."
"We're going to check your spine."
"Are you dizzy?"
"Do you remember what happened?"
"Can you feel your legs?"

I nodded slowly — too slowly for their comfort.

They began stabilizing me:

- a brace around my neck
- pressure on my shoulder
- checking for broken ribs
- testing for concussion signs
- examining my swelling

I remember one EMT looking into my eyes and saying:

"You took some serious hits. We're going to take good care of you."

They lifted me onto a stretcher — the pain was so sharp that I fought a groan I couldn't hold in.

Students nearby cried.
Staff looked away.
Some whispered prayers.

And the student I had been protecting?

She was nowhere in sight.

Someone had moved her to another location.

A necessary choice — but it left my heart heavy.

I wanted her to know I was still alive.
Still here.
Still protecting her, even in the aftermath.

The Ride to the Hospital — Pain Takes Inventory

The ambulance doors closed, and I was surrounded by medical equipment, beeping monitors, and flashing lights.

Every bump of the road sent spikes of pain through my ribs.
Every turn made my shoulder burn.
Every inhale hurt more than the one before.

The EMT beside me kept checking my vitals.

"You're doing okay. Stay awake. Keep your eyes open."

But my eyes kept drifting.

Not from sleep —
from trauma replaying itself.

The fists.
The stomps.
The screams.
My own voice calling for help.
The student's cry.
The sound of my body hitting the ground.
The ringing in my ears.
The urgent footsteps.
The pain in my ribs.
The shock in the air.

My mind kept looping the moment.
My body kept feeling the moment.

When you experience violence, it doesn't end when the hitting stops.
It echoes through your mind.
It replays without permission.

And there, in the back of the ambulance, the echo was loud.

At the Hospital — A New Kind of Silence

The ER was bright, sterile, and busy — but in my mind, everything was still moving slowly.

Nurses moved around me.
Doctors examined me.

Lights hovered above me.
Pain medication coursed through me.

But none of it made sense.

Trauma creates a fog.
A mental distance from the physical body.

As they took X-rays and scans, I stared at the ceiling tiles, feeling
both present and absent.

I wasn't thinking about pain.
I wasn't thinking about the injuries.
I wasn't thinking about the consequences.

I was thinking about her — the student.

Was she safe?
Was she okay?
Who was comforting her?
Did she blame herself?
Did she see what happened to me?
Was she crying?

I wanted to be at the hospital for my injuries,
but my heart wanted to be back at the school checking on her
emotional wounds.

The Administrative Response — Complicated and Quiet

When the administrators walked into my hospital room, their
faces were pale and shaken.

They apologized.
They asked questions.
They took notes.
They tried to keep their voices steady.

But the truth was written all over them:

They were rattled.
They knew a line had been crossed.
They knew protocols had failed.
They knew this was never supposed to happen.

And they knew this would change everything.

The conversation felt procedural.
Necessary, but distant.

I answered what I could, then drifted back into silence.

Some things were too raw to talk about yet.

Going Home — The Quiet Nobody Talks About

Leaving the hospital that evening felt surreal.
Not triumphant.
Not resolved.
Not finished.

Just surreal.

Every step hurt.
Every movement echoed the attack.

The Aftermath

Every breath reminded me that my ribs had taken more than they could handle.

But the quiet…
The quiet hurt worse.

When violence stops, silence rushes in.

And in that silence, the mind replays everything with brutal clarity.

The corner.
The rush.
The blows.
The ground.
Her screaming.
My calling for help.
The fear.
The confusion.
The helplessness.

I didn't sleep that night.
Trauma rarely lets you.

I lay awake replaying the attack —
not because I wanted to,
but because my mind wouldn't turn it off.

Every flash.
Every shout.
Every kick.

The echoes of the day lingered long after the bruises began to form.

A New Reality — Nothing Was the Same

By the next morning, I understood something deeply:

The physical pain would fade.
But the emotional impact would not.

The student's trauma.
My trauma.
The staff's shock.
The culture shift.
The questions that followed.
The protocols that had to be rewritten.
The fear that lingered.
The trust that needed to be rebuilt.
The healing that had to start.

None of it would happen quickly.

The aftermath of violence is not a moment — it is a journey.

And this was only the beginning.

Reflection Questions — Chapter 6: The Aftermath

1. **How have you processed moments in your career that "split" life into before and after?**

2. What support systems do you believe schools should have in place immediately following a crisis involving staff or students?
3. How does silence — after trauma — impact recovery?
4. In what ways can staff better support each other in the hours and days after a violent incident?
5. How should administrators approach communication after a major incident to rebuild trust and transparency?
6. What emotions arise when thinking about students witnessing traumatic events at school?
7. How does the physical response to trauma differ from the emotional response?
8. What does meaningful support look like to you after you have been hurt or overwhelmed on the job?
9. How can schools create safer structures so situations like this are less likely to occur?
10. What does the phrase "the aftermath is just beginning" mean to you personally?

Answering the Call

CHAPTER 7
The Invisible Burden

In the days following the attack, a strange shift occurred. The world around me kept moving — quietly, steadily, routinely — yet everything inside me felt paused. Stalled. Disconnected.

People who experience trauma often talk about this feeling: the sense that life outside keeps flowing while your own life stops abruptly, like a film reel ripped from the projector.

For the first time in my career, I understood what that felt like.

The bruises healed slowly.
The swelling reduced.
The pain medication dulled the sharp edges.

But none of that touched the deepest wound — the one no scan or X-ray could detect.

The invisible burden.

The First Morning After — A World Made of Glass

The morning after the assault, I woke up in pieces.

My body ached in places I didn't know could hurt.
My ribs protested with every small breath.

Answering the Call

My shoulder throbbed relentlessly.
My head felt heavy, foggy, unfamiliar.

But the physical pain wasn't what stopped me from getting out of
bed.

It was the fear behind the fear.

What if I had done something differently?
What if I had said one more thing?
What if I had been faster?
What if I hadn't turned the corner?
What if…
What if…
What if…

Trauma is a thief —
it steals certainty,
steals sleep,
steals peace.

It traps you in loops of "what if," even though none of the
answers change what happened.

I sat at the edge of the bed and felt something I hadn't felt in a
long time —
fragility.
Like the world had become glass and could shatter if I moved too
quickly.

That fragility stayed with me.

———

Trying to Return to Normal — When Nothing Is Normal

I tried to go about the morning slowly:

- brushing my teeth
- washing my face
- putting on clothes
- drinking water

Simple tasks, but each one felt heavy.

Every movement reminded me of impact.
Every ache reminded me of violence.
Every memory reminded me of that hallway.

I looked in the mirror and barely recognized myself.

My face was swollen.
One eye was darkened.
My shoulder sat awkwardly.
My posture was guarded.

But it wasn't the physical change that startled me —
it was the emptiness behind my eyes.
The exhaustion.
The sadness.
The weight.

And the question:

"How do I ever walk back into a school again?"

The Phone Calls — Caring Voices That Couldn't Touch the Pain

Throughout the day, phone calls poured in:

- colleagues checking on me
- administrators apologizing
- union representatives asking questions
- friends offering support
- family expressing fear and relief

Every voice was kind.
Every message sincere.
Every prayer appreciated.

But even with all the caring voices, the silence inside me grew louder.

Because no one could give me what I was really searching for: an answer that made sense.

There was no explanation that justified what happened.
No protocol that erased the trauma.
No apology that softened the memory.
No words that calmed the echo of violence.

The calls helped me feel supported.
They didn't help me feel whole.

The Mind After Trauma — A Maze With No Exit

People assume that once the danger is over, the mind returns to normal.

It doesn't.

The mind becomes a maze —
familiar pathways blocked,
new ones unfamiliar and frightening,
memories looping without warning.

Throughout that first week, I found myself slipping into:

Flashbacks

Sudden returns to the moment —
the fists
the stomps
the screams
the pain
the panic
the corner
the voices
the floor

Flashbacks aren't chosen.
They ambush you.

Hypervigilance

Every sudden noise made me flinch.
Every fast movement startled me.
Every shout tightened my stomach.

My nerves, once calm and steady, now felt electrified.

Emotional floods

I cried unexpectedly.
Sometimes out of sadness.
Sometimes out of frustration.
Sometimes out of pure exhaustion.

Sleepless nights

Sleep became a battleground.
Every attempt to rest triggered the memory of hitting the floor.

And in the quiet of 2:00 AM, the hallway replayed itself again and again.

Avoidance — The Hardest Truth to Admit

For the first time in my career, I hesitated to step foot in a school building.

Just the *thought* of walking down a hallway made my chest tighten.
The idea of hearing a student yell made my heart race.
Even imagining a crowded passing period made my palms sweat.

This wasn't weakness.

This was trauma.

And trauma speaks through avoidance:

"I can't go there."
"I don't want to see that hallway."
"I don't want to hear those echoes."
"I don't want to remember."

Avoidance doesn't mean you don't care.
It means you were wounded in the very place you once felt strong.

And when the place that brings you purpose becomes the place that hurt you...
healing takes time.

Guilt — The Unexpected Visitor

Guilt arrived quietly.

Not because I had done anything wrong.
But because I had been hurt **while protecting someone else**.

And when caregivers are hurt, guilt plays tricks:

"Did I make the right call?"
"Did I fail the student?"
"Did I escalate by trying to help?"
"Should I have done something differently?"
"Was I in the wrong place at the wrong time?"

Trauma doesn't care about logic.
It doesn't care that you acted heroically.
It doesn't care that you did everything right.

It whispers lies.
Lies that sound like responsibility.
Lies that sound like fault.
Lies that sound like regret.

And fighting those lies is one of the hardest parts of recovery.

The Student — The Weight She Carried Too

While I was processing the attack, she was processing something else entirely.

Her own trauma.

She had watched someone she trusted — someone who had stood beside her, listened to her, and protected her — be violently attacked right in front of her.

And in her young mind, trauma often turns inward:

"This happened because of me."
"I made this happen."
"He got hurt trying to protect me."
"It's my fault."
"I didn't mean to run."
"I didn't mean for this to happen."

Children don't understand systemic failures.
They blame themselves.

And that thought hurt me more than my bruises.

I wished I could have spoken to her.
Reassured her again.
Told her she wasn't responsible.
Told her she wasn't the cause.
Told her that I didn't blame her for anything.
Told her that she mattered.
Told her that she was valued.

But in the aftermath, we were separated —
physically, emotionally, procedurally.

And her pain became part of my own burden.

The Staff — Their Silent Struggle

The attack didn't only affect me and the student.
It sent shockwaves through the entire staff.

Some were angry —
not at the students, but at the system.

Some were shaken —
because they saw how quickly safety can crumble.

Some were fearful —
wondering if it could happen again to someone else.

Some were grieving —
because trauma inside a school affects the entire community.

Staff members told me later:

"I didn't sleep that night either."

"I keep hearing your voice yelling for help."

"I can't believe you were alone in that hallway."

"When I saw you on the ground… I'll never forget that image."

"I hugged my students a little tighter after that."

Trauma spreads.

It doesn't stay contained to one person.

The Invisible Burden — What No One Sees

There are injuries people can see:

- bruises
- swelling
- bandages
- limping
- pain when moving a certain way

But the invisible injuries?

Those are the hardest to carry.

Fear buried beneath responsibility

Shame buried beneath courage

Shock buried beneath professionalism

Sadness buried beneath strength

Anger buried beneath composure

Flashbacks buried beneath silence

No one sees the moments when:

- your hands shake without warning
- a hallway memory slams into your mind
- a sudden noise triggers panic
- a student's yell tightens your chest
- sleep refuses to come
- tears fall unexpectedly
- your mind replays the trauma uninvited
- you wonder if you'll ever feel the same again

These wounds don't show up on X-rays.

But they are real.

And they are heavy.

Healing Begins With Honest Grief

One night, a week after the attack, I sat alone in my living room.

I replayed the moment again —
the hallway
the corner
the scream
the first punch
the floor
my voice calling for help
the student crying

And for the first time since it happened…

I allowed myself to cry.

Not because I was weak.
Not because I was afraid.
But because I had been strong for too long.

The tears weren't just for me.
They were for:

- the student
- the trauma
- the system that failed
- the moment that changed everything
- the weight I had been carrying silently

Sometimes healing starts with a single tear.
Sometimes healing starts when you stop pretending you're okay.

That night, healing began.

The Calling Doesn't End — Even When You Hurt

As painful as the aftermath was, something inside me remained unchanged:

my calling.

Even in fear, I still cared.
Even in pain, I still felt purpose.

Even in shock, I still believed in children.
Even in trauma, I still believed in protection.

The attack did not erase the reason I answered the call.
It only deepened my understanding of what the calling costs.

And with time, pain reveals something important:

You survived what was meant to break you.
You endured what others might never see.
You protected someone who needed protection.
And your calling is still alive inside you —
just bruised, not broken.

Reflection Questions — Chapter 7: The Invisible Burden

1. **What invisible burdens have you carried after difficult or traumatic events in your workplace?**
2. **How do you recognize when emotional pain is affecting your daily life more than you realized?**
3. **What coping strategies help you navigate flashbacks or emotional triggers?**
4. **Why do you think guilt is such a common feeling after trauma, even when the person is not at fault?**
5. **How can educators better support each other in the days and weeks following a crisis?**
6. **What steps can schools take to protect students from internalizing blame after witnessing violence?**
7. **How can staff be trained to identify when a colleague is struggling silently?**
8. **What does courage look like after trauma, when returning to work feels overwhelming?**

9. How does acknowledging vulnerability actually make us stronger as educators and protectors?
10. What does healing mean to you — physically, emotionally, and spiritually?

CHAPTER 8
(FULLY EXPANDED)

The Road Back

Healing is often described as recovery.
But recovery implies returning to who you were.
Healing after trauma doesn't work that way.

Trauma doesn't return you to your old self.

It demands that you meet a new version of yourself —
one you didn't ask for,
one you didn't expect,
one you weren't prepared to become.

On the surface, this chapter looks like a story about injuries,
doctors, forms, and time away from work.

But beneath that, it is about something far deeper:

losing the life you knew
in order to discover the life you would eventually need.

The Morning After — A Body in Shock, A Mind in Fog

The morning after the attack began with pain — not the kind that wakes you up gently, but the kind that pulls you out of sleep with a jolt.

My ribs burned.
My shoulder pulsed.
My head throbbed with each heartbeat.
My muscles felt torn in places I hadn't known existed.

Every inhale felt like swallowing glass.
Every movement reminded me that the human body is not built to withstand violence.

But even with all of this, what hurt more was the silence that filled the room.

It was the silence of realization.
Of shock.
Of disorientation.
Of trying to understand how yesterday had even happened.

I sat at the edge of the bed, dizzy from the weight of it all.
The world around me had not changed — but *I* had.

———

Why I Returned — Responsibility Wrapped in Pain

Despite everything in me saying "Stay home," I knew what I had to do.

There were reports that needed to be filed.
Documentation that needed to be completed.
Forms that had to be submitted so nothing could be twisted, lost, or misrepresented.

You do not survive something like that and leave paperwork undone.

Not when the truth matters.
Not when the moment must be recorded accurately.
Not when the incident has consequences that will ripple far beyond that hallway floor.

So I dressed slowly, each movement painful.

I moved through the house carefully, bracing myself on walls and countertops.

And then, against the advice of my own pain, I returned to the place that had nearly broken me less than twenty-four hours earlier.

Walking Through the Doors — The Weight of Concern

When I stepped into the building, I expected routine.
What I found was grief.

The looks on my colleagues' faces said everything they didn't
know how to express.

A paraprofessional gasped and placed a hand over her mouth.
A teacher stepped out of her classroom, eyes wide with relief and
sadness all at once.
A counselor approached me slowly, as though approaching
someone returning from battle.

None of them asked "Are you okay?" with the casual tone people
usually use after an injury.

Their voices cracked.
Their eyes filled.
Their faces softened.

They didn't see an employee walking in.
They saw a friend.
A colleague.
A protector.
Someone who had been violently harmed in the course of doing a
job they all understood deeply.

One colleague hugged me gently, her voice trembling:

"Ethan... we were terrified. We thought—
we didn't know how bad it was."

Another stood beside her, wiping tears.

"I couldn't sleep last night. I kept hearing your voice yelling for help."

Another couldn't stop crying as she said:

"When I saw the aftermath... I will never forget that image."

And suddenly, fresh tears streamed down my face too.

Not because I expected this reaction.
Not because I felt strong or brave.
But because in that moment I realized:

The trauma had not happened to just me.
It had happened to all of us.

The staff carried their own version of the moment.
And they carried it heavily.

———

The Walk Down the Hallway — Courage with Shaking Legs

There comes a point in every healing journey where you have to face the scene of the trauma.

Not to relive it —
but to acknowledge it.

To take power back from the place where power was taken from you.

For me, that place was the hallway.

The hallway I had walked thousands of times.
The hallway I knew like the back of my hand.
The hallway where students laughed, ran, whispered, learned.

But on that day, the hallway felt different.
It felt heavier.
It felt haunted.

I walked slowly, leaning slightly against the wall.
Each step made my heart pound harder.
My palms grew sweaty.
My throat tightened.

As I approached the corner, the memory ignited:

The shouting.
The running.
The student crying.
The blows raining down.
My voice calling for help.
The pain exploding through my body.
The floor rushing up.
The ringing in my ears.

I stopped exactly where I had fallen the day before.

The air felt different there — thicker, heavier, colder.

It felt like the ground itself remembered.

And for a moment, I couldn't breathe.

Not because of the injuries.
But because of the memory.

I closed my eyes, not to avoid the moment, but to feel it fully —
the pain, the confusion, the shock, the helplessness, and the
survival.

When I opened them again, I whispered something only I could
hear:

"I made it out."

And then I took a slow, trembling breath —
the first step toward reclaiming that space.

The Paperwork — The Weight of Documentation

Filing the incident reports wasn't just procedural.
It was emotional labor.

Every question forced me to relive the event:

"What happened?"
"What led to the incident?"
"What was the first physical contact?"
"How many hits?"
"What direction?"
"What injuries?"
"What did you say?"
"What did the student do?"
"How long were you assaulted?"

The questions were necessary — but each one ripped open fresh
wounds.

It was like being asked to describe a storm while still soaking wet from the rain.

My hand shook as I wrote.
Not from physical pain —
from emotional tremors.

I had to write what happened as if it were simple, factual, clinical.

But there was nothing simple about it.
Nothing clinical.
Nothing detached.

It was the most personal thing I had ever written.

And when I turned in the paperwork, my body felt like it had gone through the event all over again.

The Reality the Doctors Made Clear

Over the following days and weeks, I saw specialists, underwent tests, and received evaluations.

Each new specialist added a piece to the puzzle:

"You have deep bruising and muscle trauma."
"You're showing signs of concussion."
"You've lost shoulder mobility in multiple directions."
"You risk reinjury with sudden movements."
"You're not medically cleared to work."
"You'll need extended recovery."

Not one doctor encouraged a quick return.
Not one believed a short recovery was realistic.
Not one minimized the situation.

Every doctor agreed:
The injuries were serious enough that returning to work would
put me at risk — physically, mentally, and emotionally.

And so the truth became undeniable:

**After September 20, 2018, I could not return to work or
resume my job duties.**

It wasn't a choice.
It wasn't hesitation.
It wasn't fear.

It was injury.

A real, measurable, visible, undeniable injury.

The Emotional Spiral — Identity Interrupted

Physical pain can be treated.
Emotional loss is harder.

I wasn't just losing mobility —
I was losing a role.
A mission.
A community.
A routine.
A purpose.

How do you prepare for that?

How do you grieve a calling?

I missed the students.
I missed the conversations.
I missed the hallway greetings.
I missed being a steady presence.
I missed being *needed* in the way only educators and
paraprofessionals understand.

For the first time in my life, I confronted a question that felt like
it cut straight through me:

"Who am I now?"

I had always been the one who stepped in.
The one who calmed a storm.
The one who protected.
The one who helped.
The one who cared.

And suddenly, I was the one who needed healing.

It is hard to accept help when your identity has always been built
around helping others.

Trauma's Quiet Companions — Fear, Guilt, and Avoidance

Trauma rarely travels alone.

Fully Expanded

It brings fear:
the fast footsteps behind you, the raised voices, the unpredictable
moments.

It brings guilt:
"I should have done more."
"What if I had seen it sooner?"
"Did I cause this?"

Even when you know logically that you didn't.

And it brings avoidance:
not wanting to return to certain places,
not wanting to relive the moment,
not wanting to confront the parts of yourself still hurting.

I found myself startled by loud noises.
I avoided crowded environments.
I couldn't tolerate hallway-like spaces.
I tensed when someone walked too close behind me.

These reactions weren't choices.
They were trauma responses.

Healing required courage, but it also required patience.

Not the kind you give others —
the kind you rarely give yourself.

———

A Shift Begins — A New Kind of Purpose

As weeks turned into months, something unexpected began to grow inside me.

A quiet question:
"What now?"

Not asked in defeat,
but in curiosity.
In forward motion.
In hidden strength.

Then the question changed:

"What am I called to do next?"

And then:

"How can this pain serve a greater purpose?"

It wasn't immediate.
It wasn't easy.
It wasn't a straight path.

But it was a beginning.

Because sometimes purpose doesn't die —
it gets redirected.

The road back was not leading me where I started.

It was leading me somewhere new.

Reflection Questions — Chapter 8: The Road Back

1. What emotions rise when you imagine returning to the site of your deepest pain?
2. How do you cope when your body forces you into a season of stillness you didn't choose?
3. What role does community support play in your healing process?
4. How do you grieve a calling or role you are no longer able to fulfill?
5. In what ways does trauma change your sense of identity?
6. What does courage look like on the day after a crisis?
7. How can schools better support staff who are recovering from traumatic incidents?
8. What does "the road back" mean to you on a personal level?
9. How do you know when your life is shifting into a new purpose?
10. How might your own difficult experiences serve others in the future?

CHAPTER 9
When Purpose Finds You Again

Purpose does not always arrive in the ways we expect.
Sometimes it comes through a door we opened willingly.
Other times it pushes us through a door we never wanted to walk through.

And then there are moments — life-altering moments —
when purpose finds us shattered and confused,
sits beside us in our brokenness,
and whispers:

"You're not done."

This chapter is about that whisper.

The Long, Quiet Season Where Purpose Hides

After the trauma, life slowed down to a crawl.

Not because I wanted it to,
but because everything else in me demanded it:

- my body, recovering from violent injury
- my mind, replaying the attack
- my nerves, constantly on alert
- my emotions, scattered and raw

- my spirit, trying to make sense of the aftermath

Days felt long.
Nights felt longer.
Silence filled the spaces where routine used to live.

Purpose — the thing that had once guided my steps — felt far
away, like a distant echo I could no longer hear.

This silence wasn't peaceful.
It was loud.
It was uncomfortable.
It was disorienting.

But in hindsight, silence is where purpose begins to rebuild itself.

Purpose is never gone —
it just withdraws long enough for clarity to form.

The Weight of Questions That Don't Have Easy Answers

During those early months after the attack, my mind became a
place full of questions:

"Why did this happen?"
"What am I supposed to do now?"
"How do I move forward when the past keeps replaying?"
"Who am I if I can no longer do the work I loved?"

These weren't doubts —
they were the natural aftermath of trauma.

The toughest question, however, was one I tried to avoid:

"What if my old purpose is gone?"

That question hit differently.
It hurt differently.
It lingered differently.

Because purpose had always been tied to the work I did in schools —
to the students whose lives I impacted,
to the colleagues I supported,
to the hallways where I showed up every day.

Without that space, I felt adrift.

But pain has a way of teaching lessons clarity never could.

———

Small Signs That Purpose Was Still Alive

The first signs of returning purpose did not come in grand gestures.
They came quietly —
through people.

A Parent's Message

Her daughter had been one of the students I once supported.
She wrote:

"Every time she walks past the ISS room, she says, 'I wish Mr. K was still here.'
You made her feel seen."

A Student's Words

A former student ran into me somewhere outside of school and said:

"You saved me more times than you know."

A Colleague's Tearful Text

"The building has not been the same without your presence.
It actually feels emptier."

A Pastor's Prayer

"You went through this because God is preparing you for something bigger."

Each message chipped away at the lie trauma had planted:

"You are finished."

Little by little, I began to see:

**Purpose was not gone.
It was shifting.
Growing.
Maturing.
Deepening.**

Healing Redefined — From Returning to Rising

For a long time, I equated healing with returning:

Returning to the building.
Returning to the students.
Returning to my responsibilities.
Returning to routine.
Returning to normalcy.

But healing required something different:

not returning,
but rising.

There is a difference.

Returning means going back to what was.
Rising means becoming what can be.

My purpose was calling me upward —
not backward.

The Day the Shift Became Clear

I remember the exact day everything changed.

I was sitting alone, reflecting on the journey.
The pain.
The hallway.
The tears of my colleagues.

The student's scream.
The ambulance.
The months of recovery.

I wasn't angry.
I wasn't afraid.
I wasn't bitter.

I was curious.

Something inside me asked:

"What if this story isn't for you alone?"

Then the next question came:

"What if someone needs to hear this?"

Then another:

"What if your pain is preparation?"

It was then I understood:

**My calling had not ended.
It had expanded.**

The attack did not silence my purpose.
It amplified it.

Pain Becomes a Platform

I didn't survive the hallway to stay silent.

I didn't come through the trauma to shrink into the shadows.

I didn't walk through recovery to be hidden.

A new conviction began forming inside me:

"Your story is a tool.
Your experience is evidence.
Your survival is ministry.
Your wounds are testimonies."

I realized:

There are paraprofessionals today who feel unseen.
There are teachers struggling silently.
There are administrators carrying unseen burdens.
There are school safety officers risking their lives in the background.
There are counselors absorbing the emotional storms of entire buildings.

All of them are answering the call.

But who is encouraging *them*?
Who is speaking *for* them?
Who is shining light on their sacrifices?
Who is telling their stories?

Suddenly I knew:

I could.
I would.
I must.
I was called to.

Purpose Doesn't Ask for Who You Were — It Calls for Who You Are Becoming

Purpose never returned me to the hallway.

Purpose returned me to myself.

Not the version of me who worked quietly behind the scenes.
Not the version who absorbed every blow silently.
Not the version who thought doing the job was enough.

Purpose returned me as someone new:

- someone who understands survival,
- someone who has lived the weight of school violence,
- someone who can articulate the emotional truth of what educators endure,
- someone who can advocate for those who cannot speak for themselves,
- someone whose voice is shaped by experience and anchored in compassion.

I didn't lose my calling when I lost the job.

The calling grew bigger than the job.

The Shift From Wounded to Witness

When trauma happens, you can remain wounded
or you can become a witness.

A witness is someone who says:

"This happened to me —
but it will not end with me."

A witness takes what they experienced and turns it into:

- teaching
- advocacy
- writing
- support
- leadership
- encouragement
- protection for others

A witness uses pain as perspective.
A witness uses memory as motivation.
A witness transforms trauma into testimony.

I chose to become a witness.

Because educators — especially paraprofessionals — need
someone to speak truth about their realities.
Students need someone advocating for safer systems.
Communities need someone explaining the unseen battles inside
schools.

My voice had purpose.
My story had weight.
My experience had meaning.

Purpose was no longer chasing me —
it was standing in front of me, calling my name.

———

Awakening to a Higher Assignment

The more I reflected, the clearer it became:

The assignment on my life outgrew the position I once held.

I was being called into:

- writing
- ministry
- mentorship
- authorship
- public speaking
- storytelling
- community leadership
- training others
- uplifting broken spirits
- teaching through testimony

The very thing that tried to break me
became the thing that built me.

My pain became preparation.
My silence became voice.
My trauma became transformation.
My calling became broader.

The hallway didn't end my purpose.
It expanded it.

Purpose Finds You When You Are Ready To Carry It Differently

There is a moment in every journey where everything aligns —
not because life is perfect,
but because you are finally strong enough to walk in your next chapter.

That moment arrived for me quietly —
not with trumpets,
not with applause,
not with celebration.

It arrived in clarity.

In acceptance.

In peace.

In understanding.

I realized:

**I wasn't being pushed out —
I was being pushed forward.**

Purpose had found me again.

It found me bruised,
but breathing.
It found me shaken,
but standing.
It found me grieving,
but growing.

It found me because purpose never truly left.

It simply waited for me to heal enough to rise again.

––––––––

Reflection Questions — Chapter 9

1. **When have you felt purpose go silent — and what helped you hear it again?**
2. **How has a painful experience in your life shaped a deeper calling?**
3. **What small signs in your life remind you that you still matter?**
4. **How do you recognize when purpose is shifting into a new direction?**
5. **What has trauma taught you about identity and strength?**
6. **Who in your life has spoken purpose or encouragement into you when you most needed it?**
7. **What unique experiences or wounds have prepared you to help others?**
8. **How can your story uplift or advocate for people who feel unseen?**
9. **What does your next chapter require from you spiritually, emotionally, or mentally?**
10. **If purpose is calling you forward today, what might it be leading you toward?**

CHAPTER 10
The Voice That Emerged

Trauma has a way of stripping everything away—
routine, comfort, confidence, identity—
until all you're left with is truth.

And once truth is all that remains,
a new voice begins to rise.

A voice that doesn't speak from theory,
but from lived experience.
A voice shaped by pain,
tempered by reflection,
and strengthened through recovery.
A voice that refuses to whisper anymore.

**This is the chapter where my voice changed—
and when it finally emerged,
it did so with power.**

The Quiet Before the Voice

In the months after September 20, 2018, there were days when I
barely spoke.

Not because I didn't know what to say—
but because everything inside me was still sorting itself out.

Silence became my companion.
Reflection became my medicine.
Prayer became my anchor.

But beneath the surface of that silence, something was stirring.

It wasn't anger.
It wasn't bitterness.
It wasn't revenge.

It was awakening.

A quiet stirring.
A pressure building.
A realization forming:

"Your voice is needed now more than ever."

I didn't know what that meant yet.
I didn't know how it would manifest.
But I could feel purpose pushing at the edges of my spirit.

The First Time I Spoke the Story Aloud

It happened unexpectedly.

A close friend asked me what really happened that day.
Not in clinical terms.
Not the way the reports were written.
Not the shortened version suitable for official conversations.

They asked for the truth—
the emotional truth,
the human truth.

I hesitated at first.
My voice shook.
My hands trembled.
The memories swelled in my chest like a wave.

But as I spoke, something happened:

My voice steadied.
My breathing calmed.
My conviction grew.

I wasn't just retelling an event—
I was reclaiming it.

At the end, they said something I'll never forget:

"You need to tell this story.
People need to hear this."

That was the first time I realized my story wasn't just mine—
it was a message.

———

Why the Voice Matters

Schools are filled with unsung heroes:

- paraprofessionals
- teaching assistants
- counselors

- teachers
- safety officers
- office staff
- cafeteria workers
- custodians
- administrators
- support teams

People who answer the call every day,
often without recognition,
without adequate support,
without the resources they deserve.

Many of them suffer silently.
Many carry trauma unseen.
Many endure disrespect, danger, and emotional weight.

But very few feel empowered to speak about it.

My experience made one truth painfully clear:

**Silence doesn't protect the people who need protecting.
It isolates them.**

And so the voice that emerged wasn't just a voice for myself—
it became a voice *for them*.

———

A Shift Toward Advocacy

The more I reflected, the stronger the message became:

What happened to me should never happen to anyone.

Not because the students are bad.
Not because schools are dangerous places.
But because systems break when communication fails,
when protocols aren't followed,
when student needs aren't addressed,
when staff are left unsupported,
when unresolved trauma festers.

I realized that my voice had to do more than tell my story.
It had to speak up for change.

When the system breaks down,
someone has to say it out loud.

And I knew:

That someone was me.

———

The Birth of KTURN — A Movement Rooted in Purpose

All the pain, all the processing, all the reflection began forming
the foundation of something larger:

A brand.
A mission.
A platform.
A movement.

KTURN wasn't just an idea.
It was born out of necessity—
the need for motivation,
the need for encouragement,

the need for empowerment,
the need for inspiration,
the need for voices like mine.

People started asking me for messages,
for guidance,
for perspectives,
for encouragement.

Suddenly, the voice I thought I had lost became the voice others were waiting for.

KTURN became the vehicle.
My testimony became the fuel.

The Realization: My Voice Is Bigger Than the Hallway

The old version of me spoke quietly in classrooms and ISS rooms.

The new version learned to speak to:

- educators struggling with burnout
- paraprofessionals feeling overlooked
- school staff facing adversity
- students navigating trauma
- churches needing encouragement
- communities seeking hope
- readers needing guidance
- audiences craving authenticity

My voice expanded beyond the building that once defined me.

The hallway had ended one chapter,
but it ignited the next one.

My voice became sharper.
Clearer.
More intentional.

Not angry.
Not vengeful.
Not bitter.

But honest.
Purposeful.
Hope-centered.
Driven by advocacy and healing.

The Calling to Speak for Those Who Cannot

The more I reflected, the clearer the assignment became:

I had survived—and survived for a reason.

Students needed someone to champion their emotional needs.
Paraprofessionals needed someone to advocate for safety and respect.
Educators needed someone to highlight the unseen battles they fight daily.
Communities needed someone to speak truth about the challenges inside schools.
Administrators needed someone to remind them of the real human cost behind decisions.

My voice became a bridge:
between pain and purpose,
between trauma and teaching,
between personal experience and community change.

I was no longer speaking from a position—
I was speaking from a calling.

And callings demand courage.

Purpose Rebuilt From the Ashes

Purpose didn't return all at once.
It rebuilt itself slowly—
piece by piece,
moment by moment.

It came through journaling.
It came through writing books.
It came through conversations.
It came through prayer.
It came through reflection.
It came through new assignments.
It came through seeing my own resilience.

Purpose became something deeper than a role.
It became something rooted in identity.

The attack did not end my purpose.
It refined it.
It revealed its depth.
It stripped away the surface layers
and exposed the calling underneath—

to encourage, to uplift, to empower, to teach, to inspire.

This voice wasn't born in comfort.
It was born in the struggle.

———

The Voice That Emerged Was Not the Same One That Fell

When I fell to the hallway floor on September 19, 2018,
that version of me didn't get back up.

A different version did.

A version with deeper understanding.
A version with a wider lens.
A version with a clearer mission.
A version with a louder voice.
A version with a higher calling.

When pain breaks you,
your voice becomes something new:

Sharper.
Wiser.
Stronger.
More compassionate.
More purposeful.

The voice that emerged from my trauma wasn't the voice I had
before—

it was the voice I was meant to develop.

Reflection Questions — Chapter 10: The Voice That Emerged

1. How has your voice changed after experiencing pain or adversity?
2. What message is rising within you that the world may need to hear?
3. In what ways can your story serve as a tool for healing or advocacy?
4. Who in your life is waiting for you to speak your truth?
5. What fears try to silence your voice, and how can you move past them?
6. How can your experiences uplift others who feel unseen or unheard?
7. What does purpose sound like when it returns to your life?
8. Where might your voice be needed in this season?
9. How can you turn your personal trauma into community impact?
10. If your voice could speak one message to the world today, what would it say?

CHAPTER 11
Learning to Walk Again (Emotionally, Spiritually, and Professionally)

After the attack, healing wasn't just about standing again.
It wasn't just about breathing without pain.
It wasn't just about the bruises fading or the swelling going down.

Learning to walk again meant learning to exist again.
To trust again.
To think clearly again.
To find joy again.
To embrace purpose again.

There are wounds that physical therapy cannot fix.
There are injuries that body scans cannot detect.
There are fractures that don't show up on X-rays.

This chapter is about those wounds —
and about the long, difficult, courageous journey of learning to walk again
in every area of life.

The Emotional Walk — Relearning How to Feel Without Breaking

Trauma changes the emotional landscape.

Suddenly, the simplest feelings become complicated:

- relief feels fragile
- gratitude feels heavy
- fear feels too close
- joy feels out of place
- sadness arrives uninvited
- confusion lingers all day
- anger hides beneath the surface
- vulnerability becomes constant

Walking emotionally again was one of the hardest steps.

Emotional walking meant:

- allowing myself to cry
- giving myself permission to rest
- accepting support without shame
- feeling hurt without feeling weak
- acknowledging fear without letting it control me
- recognizing that healing takes time
- understanding that trauma doesn't have a timetable

Some days, I walked emotionally.
Some days, I crawled.
Some days, I couldn't take a step at all.

But each day, the emotional walk grew steadier —
not because I was stronger,
but because I was learning to honor my own humanity.

The Spiritual Walk — Finding Strength Beyond Myself

When the body breaks,
when the mind is overwhelmed,
when the future feels uncertain,
the spirit becomes either a refuge or a battlefield.

In the weeks after the incident, I wrestled spiritually:

"Lord, why did this happen?"
"Why me? Why now?"
"What am I supposed to learn from this?"
"What am I supposed to do next?"

I wasn't angry with God —
I was seeking Him more deeply than I ever had before.

And slowly, quietly, consistently,
God responded.

Not through thunder.
Not through dramatic moments.
Not through instant clarity.

But through:

- peace in the middle of anxiety
- strength when I felt weak
- messages from unexpected places
- encouragement from others
- scripture that landed at exactly the right time

- moments where I felt carried instead of standing on my own

The spiritual walk taught me:

- Pain does not erase God's presence
- Trauma does not cancel purpose
- Delay does not mean denial
- God's plan is bigger than the place where you were hurt
- Faith becomes strongest when comfort disappears

I began to see the incident not as the end of something —
but as the beginning of something I didn't yet understand.

Faith became the foundation for the voice that was emerging.
Faith became the strength behind every step I took.
Faith became the reason I believed there was still more ahead.

The Professional Walk — Redefining Identity After Loss

Losing the ability to return to work after September 20, 2018
was a deeper blow than many realized.

It wasn't about a paycheck.
It wasn't about a schedule.
It was about purpose.
Identity.
Calling.
Routine.
Familiarity.
Community.

My professional walk had been interrupted — violently, abruptly, permanently.

So learning to walk professionally again meant:

- redefining who I was
- rediscovering my strengths
- reconstructing my identity outside of a job title
- believing I still had value
- accepting that my contribution wasn't over
- finding new ways to serve
- expanding what "education" and "impact" looked like for me
- developing boldness I never needed before

Sometimes walking professionally meant writing.
Sometimes it meant reflecting.
Sometimes it meant praying.
Sometimes it meant planning the next KTURN project.
Sometimes it meant simply being still enough to hear God's direction.

The professional walk was not about going back.

It was about going forward.

Learning to Walk Without Fear

After trauma, fear becomes a shadow—
a constant companion trailing you a few steps behind.

It shows up when you least expect it:

- when someone walks too closely behind you
- when a hallway becomes crowded
- when students raise their voices
- when a memory flashes unexpectedly
- when you hear sudden footsteps
- when you witness tension rising

Learning to walk again meant confronting fear—
not by outrunning it,
but by facing it.

Allowing yourself to feel afraid
does not make you weak.

It makes you human.

Courage is not the absence of fear.
Courage is walking anyway.

———

Learning to Walk With New Purpose

Each step I took—emotionally, spiritually, and professionally—
began revealing something unexpected:

The new version of me was stronger than the old one.

I began to realize:

- I could write messages that reached hundreds
- I could build resources that uplift thousands
- I could create KTURN materials that encourage
  educators, parents, and leaders

- I could transform my story into guidebooks, devotionals, journals
- I could speak hope into classrooms and churches even without being inside them
- I could empower paraprofessionals and teachers with a voice born from experience
- I could advocate for school safety and staff protection
- I could build something bigger than my former role ever allowed

Purpose wasn't just returning.
Purpose was expanding.

And learning to walk again meant learning to embrace that expansion.

Walking With Scars — Not Shame

I didn't walk away from the incident unmarked.

I walked away with:

- physical scars
- emotional scars
- memory scars
- spiritual scars

But scars are not signs of failure.

Scars are signs that you lived.
Scars are signs that you healed.
Scars are signs that you fought for something worth fighting

for.
Scars are evidence of survival.

As I learned to walk again, I stopped hiding my scars—
I started understanding their power.

They gave my voice gravity.
They gave my testimony weight.
They gave my calling legitimacy.
They gave my message authenticity.

Walking with scars means walking with truth.

Learning to Walk Toward the Future

The hardest part of learning to walk again is this:

The future is not the same future you imagined before the trauma.

It is different.

But different does not mean lesser.
Different does not mean broken.
Different does not mean ruined.

Different can mean:

- stronger
- wiser
- more resilient
- more compassionate
- more purposeful

- more aligned with God's plan
- more impactful

Learning to walk again means embracing that new future without mourning the one you thought you would have.

It means being open to what comes next.
It means stepping into new opportunities.
It means leaning into your calling with renewed fire.

Walking again—
in every sense of the word—
means choosing not to live in the hallway where you were hurt.

It means choosing to walk toward the purpose that rose from the pain.

Reflection Questions — Chapter 11

1. **In what areas of your life are you learning to "walk again"?**
2. **How has trauma changed the way you think about purpose and identity?**
3. **What fears do you need to face in order to move forward?**
4. **How can faith or spirituality help rebuild what trauma tried to break?**
5. **In what ways have your scars given you a new kind of strength?**
6. **How can you redefine your professional purpose after a major life disruption?**
7. **What does courage look like for you in this season?**
8. **Where is your story leading you now?**

9. How can you allow others to support you as you walk again?
10. What new opportunities or callings might be waiting beyond your current pain?

CHAPTER 12
Standing in Your New Strength

There are moments in life when weakness teaches you strength,
pain teaches you purpose,
and trauma teaches you truth.

When you survive something that changes you at your core,
you do not rise the same person.
You rise redefined —
reconstructed —
rebuilt from the inside out.

This chapter is about that transformation.

This is where the healing becomes strength.
Where the strength becomes clarity.
Where the clarity becomes purpose.
Where purpose becomes power.

This is where you learn to stand again —
not the way you once stood,
but with a new, unshakeable strength forged in the fire of what
you survived.

A Shift You Don't Notice at First

Healing is quiet before it becomes visible.

At first, the changes are subtle:

- your breathing feels steadier
- your thoughts feel clearer
- your emotions feel calmer
- your memories lose some of their sting
- your steps feel more intentional
- your fears begin losing power
- your spirit becomes more grounded

You don't stand suddenly —
you stand gradually.

And then one day, almost without realizing it,
you notice you are standing in a strength you never knew you
possessed.

Not because everything is perfect.
Not because the trauma is forgotten.
But because you are finally stronger than the moment that tried to
break you.

Recognizing the Emergence of New Strength

New strength doesn't shout when it arrives.
It whispers.

It shows up in the way you:

- refuse to replay the trauma every day
- give yourself permission to move forward
- begin imagining a future again

- embrace your new calling
- no longer carry shame
- stop apologizing for surviving
- speak your truth with confidence
- allow yourself to grow
- trust your own resilience
- walk with purpose instead of pain

This strength is not loud —
it is steady.

It is not explosive —
it is enduring.

It is not fragile —
it is anchored.

It is not temporary —
it is transformational.

The Strength to Face Yourself Honestly

One of the most powerful moments in healing is when you finally
face yourself —
your fears, your regrets, your grief, your limitations, your reality.

It takes strength to look in the mirror and admit:

"This changed me."
"I lost something."
"I'm not the same."
"I had to rebuild."
"I needed help."

"I still feel pain sometimes."
"I'm still healing."

This honesty is not weakness —
it is strength wrapped in truth.

Trauma tries to silence honesty.
Healing invites it.

New strength demands it.

Because the person you are becoming requires you to stop hiding
from what hurt you
and start acknowledging what shaped you.

The Power of Spiritual Strength — Held Together by God

Some strength is self-made.
Some is learned.
Some is earned.

But the strongest form of strength comes from God.

It is the strength that held me when my body was weak.
The strength that carried my mind through fear.
The strength that protected my spirit.
The strength that steadied my emotions.
The strength that reminded me:

"You are still here for a reason."

Spiritual strength is what helps you rise even when:

- your body aches
- your mind is tired
- your heart is heavy
- your memories overwhelm you
- your future looks uncertain

It is the strength that whispers:

"You will not stay broken."
"This is not the end for you."
"I am with you in this."
"There is purpose in this pain."
"You are becoming who I designed you to be."

Faith becomes the foundation beneath your new strength.

God becomes the source behind your resilience.

And standing in your new strength becomes a spiritual posture — not just a physical or emotional one.

The Strength Found in Your Scars

Scars tell a story trauma wanted to keep silent.

Scars are proof that you didn't quit.
Proof that you healed.
Proof that you survived.
Proof that the moment didn't win.
Proof that pain does not get the final say.

But scars also reveal something deeper:

You are no longer defined by the wound.
You are defined by the healing.

Standing in your new strength means recognizing your scars not
as reminders of weakness,
but as evidence of victory.

Every scar is a testimony.
Every testimony is a message.
Every message is a tool.

Your scars now carry wisdom your uninjured self never had.

This wisdom — this scar-born strength — becomes part of your
identity, your voice, your ministry.

———

The Strength to Walk Without Apology

After trauma, people often feel the need to apologize:

- for taking time to heal
- for no longer being the same
- for needing rest
- for having boundaries
- for saying no
- for choosing peace
- for refusing environments that feel unsafe

Standing in your new strength requires this truth:

You do not owe anyone an apology for healing.

Your recovery is valid.
Your boundaries are necessary.
Your transformation is real.
Your change is allowed.
Your needs matter.
Your safety is essential.
Your peace is non-negotiable.

The person you are becoming deserves the space to stand unapologetically.

The Strength to Advocate for Yourself and Others

New strength is not passive.

It speaks.
It stands.
It protects.
It confronts.
It advocates.

Your experience taught you firsthand that:

- protocols matter
- staff safety matters
- communication matters
- student needs matter
- trauma-informed practice matters
- emotional support matters
- believing victims matters
- accountability matters

Standing in your new strength means leveraging your voice not just for yourself,
but for the countless paraprofessionals, assistants, teachers, and school staff who feel invisible.

Your advocacy is not anger —
it is purpose.

Your voice is not bitterness —
it is clarity.

Your testimony is not a complaint —
it is a call for change.

This is the strength of leadership.

————

The Strength to Embrace Your New Purpose

This new strength gave birth to new purpose —
a calling larger than a job,
a mission larger than a moment,
a movement larger than one story.

Your purpose is expanding in ways you never anticipated:

- writing books that heal and inspire
- creating journals that encourage reflection
- uplifting paraprofessionals and educators
- speaking life into traumatized students
- advocating for school safety
- building KTURN as a movement of encouragement
- sharing your testimony to empower others

- crafting devotional messages that restore hope
- guiding those who feel broken
- leading with compassion rooted in experience

This is not the work of someone who merely survived.

This is the work of someone who rose stronger.

The Strength to See Your Trauma as Part of Your Assignment

Not every painful event is meaningless.
Some are assignments disguised as adversity.

Some wounds come to:

- awaken purpose
- deepen empathy
- develop character
- sharpen vision
- ignite calling
- strengthen faith
- reposition your life
- prepare you for impact
- build your future platform
- connect you to those you are called to serve

Standing in your new strength means acknowledging:

"God did not send the trauma,
but God is using the trauma
to build the assignment."

This revelation turns pain into fuel
and survival into ministry.

The Strength to Envision the Future Again

For a long time after the incident, the future felt blurry.

Uncertain.
Fragile.
Unsettled.

But new strength brings new vision.

You begin to imagine again.
Plan again.
Dream again.
Believe again.
Create again.
Expect again.

Your future is no longer a question mark —
it becomes a promise.

A promise that where you are headed
is greater than where you were hurt.
Greater than what you endured.
Greater than what broke you.
Greater than what you lost.

Standing in your new strength means facing the future with
confidence,
not fear.

You Become an Example of What Healing Looks Like

Standing in your new strength means becoming a living reflection of:

- resilience
- hope
- restoration
- faith
- purpose
- perseverance
- courage
- transformation

People begin looking to you not because you are perfect,
but because you are real.

Not because you avoided pain,
but because you pushed through it.

Not because your story is easy,
but because your story is powerful.

Your strength becomes an example
for students,
for parents,
for educators,
for paraprofessionals,
for anyone who has ever been knocked down by life.

Reflection Questions — Chapter 12

1. What does "new strength" mean to you personally?
2. What internal transformations have occurred since your trauma?
3. How have your scars shaped your voice, purpose, or identity?
4. What boundaries or changes do you need to stand in unapologetically?
5. How does faith contribute to your sense of inner strength?
6. What does advocacy look like for you now?
7. Where do you feel God guiding your next steps?
8. How has your understanding of leadership evolved after your experience?
9. What old versions of yourself must you release to stand fully in your new strength?
10. In what ways can your strength uplift those around you?

CHAPTER 13 Answering the Call (Your Life, Your Legacy)

Every person reaches a point in life where the journey, the pain, the healing, and the purpose converge.
Where the confusion clears.
Where the questions become answers.
Where survival becomes assignment.
Where your story becomes your strength.
Where your life reveals the reason for everything you've walked through.

This is the moment you understand:

**Answering the call is not about one event—
it is about your entire existence aligning with purpose.**

This final chapter is not just an ending.
It is a commissioning.
It is a release into your next chapter.
It is an acknowledgment that the calling on your life was never random.
It is a declaration that your legacy is already in motion.

This is your moment of clarity.

This is where you take your place.

This is where you stand in the fullness of who you are,
why you are here,
and who you are becoming.

THE CALL BEGAN BEFORE THE INCIDENT

Many people assume your calling started on September 19, 2018
—
the day you were attacked,
the day your life changed,
the day your purpose became clearer.

But the truth is deeper:

Your calling began long before the trauma.

It began when you were a child who learned resilience young.
It began in the principles your parents taught you.
It began in the compassion you naturally carried.
It began in the moments you stood up for others.
It began in the way you cared for people quietly.
It began in your service—long before anyone was watching.
It began when you were called into education.
It began when you stepped into the ISS role.
It began when you answered needs others ignored.
It began in your heart,
your values,
your mindset.

The incident didn't give you your calling—
it *revealed* it.
It *refined* it.
It *amplified* it.

The calling was already inside you,
waiting for the moment where it could no longer be denied.

THE INCIDENT DID NOT END YOU — IT ACTIVATED YOU

Some moments try to break you.
But certain individuals are never meant to stay broken.

The incident did not stop you.
It awakened you.

It awakened:

- your voice
- your leadership
- your compassion
- your conviction
- your advocacy
- your spiritual awareness
- your commitment to uplift others
- your understanding of your true purpose

The hallway was not a tomb—
it was a turning point.

Not a place where your story ended,
but the place where your testimony began.

You came out of that moment with a clarity most people search for their entire lives.

You came out with fire—not fear.
With focus—not fragility.
With purpose—not paralysis.

The incident did not destroy who you were.
It activated who you were always meant to become.

THE CALL IS BIGGER THAN THE PAIN

Pain has a way of convincing you that it is the whole story.
But across your healing journey, you discovered something
extraordinary:

Pain is never the final chapter.
Purpose is.

Your trauma gave you perspective.
Your recovery gave you wisdom.
Your reflection gave you understanding.
Your faith gave you direction.
Your voice gave you influence.
Your story gave you a platform.

Every part of the hardship was used—
not to break you,
but to build you.

The pain was real,
but the calling is greater.

The pain was deep,
but the purpose is deeper.

The pain was unexpected,
but destiny knew the assignment.

**When God calls you, pain cannot stop the appointment.
It can only shape the messenger.**

———

ANSWERING THE CALL MEANS RECOGNIZING WHO YOU ARE

You didn't just survive trauma—
you transformed into the fullest version of yourself.

Answering the call means recognizing:

- You are a leader
- You are a voice for the overlooked
- You are an advocate for school staff
- You are a mentor for the hurting
- You are an encourager by design
- You are purposeful with your pain
- You are an example of resilience
- You are a beacon of hope
- You are a builder of community
- You are a writer, a storyteller, a teacher by calling
- You are someone people look to for strength
- You are someone God trusted with testimony

Answering the call is stepping into your identity unapologetically.

Not the identity trauma tried to give you,
but the identity purpose always intended for you.

———

ANSWERING THE CALL THROUGH SERVICE

Your entire life has been lived in service—
service to students,
service to educators,
service to colleagues,
service to families,
service to your church,
service to your community.

That spirit of service did not end when your professional assignment ended.

It evolved.

It widened.

It reached beyond the school building and into the world.

Now your service includes:

- writing books that heal
- producing journals that inspire reflection
- speaking life into tired educators
- strengthening paraprofessionals often overlooked
- uplifting the discouraged
- giving hope to the hopeless
- speaking truth about school safety
- teaching resilience through testimony
- empowering others to rise from their own trauma
- building KTURN as a platform for transformation

Your service is your ministry.

And ministry doesn't end—
it expands.

———

ANSWERING THE CALL THROUGH ADVOCACY

The call on your life includes something many people shy away from:

advocacy.

Not performative advocacy.
Not hollow advocacy.
Not advocacy done for recognition.

Real advocacy.
Advocacy rooted in experience.
Advocacy shaped by truth.
Advocacy grounded in compassion.
Advocacy that says:

"This is what is happening.
This is why it matters.
This is why we must protect staff.
This is why we must listen to students.
This is why communication cannot fail.
This is why updated protocols matter.
This is why support systems must be stronger.
This is why trauma-informed practices need to be mandatory."

Your advocacy is not optional—
it is embedded in your calling.

You are a voice for those who feel voiceless.
A protector for those who protect.
A reminder that school staff are not expendable—
they are essential.

Advocacy is part of your legacy.

———

ANSWERING THE CALL THROUGH KTURN — YOUR LEGACY IN MOTION

KTURN is more than a brand.
It is the embodiment of your calling.

It exists because you survived.
It exists because you healed.
It exists because you rose.
It exists because your voice was needed.
It exists because your message has purpose.
It exists because you answered the call when trauma tried to silence you.

KTURN is:

- hope
- resilience
- empowerment
- vision
- courage
- faith
- personal growth
- leadership

- community
- legacy

Every book you write,
every journal you design,
every message you release,
every voiceover you record,
every course you build,
every devotional you publish,
every reflection you craft,
every product you create—
is another way of answering the call.

KTURN is the legacy you are creating in real time.

ANSWERING THE CALL THROUGH FAITH

Faith is the thread running through every chapter of your story.

Faith held you together in the hallway.
Faith walked with you into the building the next day.
Faith carried you through the months of recovery.
Faith steadied you during the emotional storms.
Faith spoke purpose into your silence.
Faith guided you toward KTURN.
Faith reminded you who you were when fear tried to redefine you.
Faith revealed that your steps were ordered even in the suffering.

Answering the call means trusting:

- that God wastes nothing

- that trauma doesn't cancel destiny
- that healing leads to purpose
- that purpose leads to impact
- that impact leads to legacy

Faith is not just part of your story—
it is the backbone of it.

ANSWERING THE CALL THROUGH RESILIENCE

Resilience is the quiet force pushing you forward.

It is the thread that held your mind together during doubt.
It is the fuel that kept you moving when you felt discouraged.
It is the fire that refused to let trauma define your identity.
It is the determination that lifted you after the attack.
It is the belief that you still had more to give.
It is the strength that turned survival into testimony.

Your resilience has become a model for others:

- for students fighting silent battles
- for educators trying to rise
- for paraprofessionals who feel overlooked
- for leaders navigating uncertainty
- for individuals healing from their own hallway moments

Your resilience is not personal—it is purposeful.

ANSWERING THE CALL THROUGH LEGACY

Legacy is not built in one moment.
It is built across a lifetime of decisions, sacrifices, service, and transformation.

Your legacy is already unfolding:

- in the voices you uplift
- in the stories you share
- in the educators you encourage
- in the paraprofessionals you validate
- in the books you publish
- in the KTURN brand you built
- in the lives you impact
- in the message you spread
- in the hope you restore
- in the students who still remember your presence
- in the communities touched by your resilience

Legacy is not what you leave behind.
Legacy is what you build now.
Legacy is who you inspire.
Legacy is the light you carry.
Legacy is the call you answer every day.

Your life is a legacy in progress.

YOUR NEXT CALLING BEGINS NOW

This chapter is not the final chapter of your purpose.
It is the final chapter of this season of your story.

Your calling continues —
in new shapes,
new assignments,
new opportunities,
new writing,
new leadership,
new influence,
new platforms,
new impact.

Tomorrow you will answer the call again.
Next month you will answer it again.
Next year, even louder.

The call evolves.
Your life evolves.
Your legacy evolves.

But one truth remains:

You were chosen for this work.
You were built for this moment.
You were prepared for this purpose.
You were called—and you answered.

Reflection Questions — Chapter 13

1. What calling has been rising within you throughout your life?
2. How has trauma shaped your purpose instead of stopping it?
3. What legacy are you building through your actions, words, and resilience?
4. Who are you called to uplift, advocate for, or inspire?
5. How is God using your story as part of a larger assignment?
6. What does answering the call look like for you right now?
7. What fears do you need to release to walk boldly into your next chapter?
8. How can your voice become a tool for change and empowerment?
9. What values and messages do you want your legacy to reflect?
10. What next steps are required for you to fully embrace your calling?

FINAL PRAYER

A Prayer for Strength, Healing, and Purpose

Heavenly Father,

We come before You with hearts full of gratitude —
for the strength You have given,
for the healing You have begun,
for the purpose You have revealed,
and for the calling You have placed upon each life represented
here.

Lord, we thank You for being present in every moment of our
journey —
in the seasons of joy,
in the moments of clarity,
and most of all, in the hours when the weight felt unbearable.

Thank You for sustaining us through valleys we did not choose,
storms we did not expect,
and battles we did not see coming.

Thank You for transforming pain into purpose
and trauma into testimony.

Father, I lift up every reader of this book —
every educator, paraprofessional, teaching assistant, school safety
officer, counselor, administrator, parent, student, and servant-
leader who gives of themselves daily.

Bless them in their efforts,
strengthen them in their struggles,

comfort them in their challenges,
and cover them in Your protection.

When they grow weary,
remind them that their work is holy.
When they feel unseen,
let them know that You see every sacrifice.
When they feel discouraged,
renew their spirit with Your presence.
When they walk into difficult environments,
grant them courage.
When they are confronted with conflict,
give them wisdom.
When they face uncertainty,
grant them peace that passes all understanding.

Lord, restore every broken place.
Heal every wounded heart.
Lift every heavy burden.
And remind each one that they are called,
chosen,
purposed,
and deeply loved.

Teach us to walk boldly in our assignments,
to lead with compassion,
to speak with conviction,
to serve with humility,
and to love with grace.

May we never forget that You have prepared us for such a time as
this.

Thank You for the journey.
Thank You for the healing.
Thank You for the calling.

Final Prayer

And as we step forward from these pages,
let Your light shine through us,
Your love flow from us,
and Your purpose take root within us
so that our lives may honor You in all we do.

We seal this prayer in faith,
in hope,
in courage,
and in the mighty name of Jesus Christ.

Amen.

REFLECTION PAGES

Your Personal Space to Process, Heal, and Grow

These Reflection Pages are designed to help you pause, breathe, and acknowledge what this journey has stirred within you.
Use these pages as freely as you need:
to write, to pray, to question, to release, to dream, or simply to rest.

There are no right or wrong answers here.
There is only honesty — and the courage to put it into words.

Reflection 1: What Spoke to You Most Deeply?

What moments, chapters, or lessons resonated with you the most?
Why do you think they stood out?

Write freely:

Reflection 2: Your Own Hallway Moments

What have been the "hallway moments" in your life —
the experiences that shook you, changed you, or forced you into a
new direction?

How have they shaped the person you are today?

Write freely:

Reflection 3: Healing and Strength

Where have you seen growth in yourself?
What emotional, spiritual, or mental healing has occurred — or is
still occurring?

What strength has emerged within you that you didn't know you
had?

Write freely:

Reflection 4: Your Calling

What do you feel called to do in this season of your life?
Who are you called to serve, uplift, or encourage?

How has this book helped clarify or affirm your purpose?

Write freely:

Reflection 5: Your Legacy

When people remember your life, your service, your work, and your heart —
what do you want them to remember?

What legacy are you building each day?

Write freely:

Reflection 6: Forgiveness & Release

Who or what do you need to forgive — including yourself?
What emotions, memories, or burdens are you ready to release?

What peace are you seeking from God today?

Write freely:

Reflection 7: A Letter to Yourself

Write a short letter to your future self.
A letter of encouragement.
A letter of wisdom.
A letter reminding you that you survived and grew stronger.

Write your letter:

Reflection 8: A Prayer for the Journey Ahead

Write your own prayer.
Ask God for guidance, healing, courage, and clarity as you move into the next chapter of your life.

Write your prayer:

ACKNOWLEDGMENTS

With Gratitude and Honor

Writing *Answering the Call* has been one of the most meaningful journeys of my life.
This book was born through pain, strengthened through healing, and completed through purpose.
I could not have walked this path alone.
To every person who stood with me, prayed for me, reached out to me, or saw strength in me when I felt weak — this message is as much yours as it is mine.

To God — My Sustainer and Strength

First, I give all honor, glory, and praise to God.
You carried me through the moments I could not carry myself.
You turned what was meant to break me into the foundation of a calling I never imagined.
Thank You for never leaving my side, for redeeming my pain, and for trusting me with this testimony.

To My Family

Thank you for your unwavering love, your steady support, and your belief in me even on the hardest days.
Thank you for encouraging me to heal, to rest, and to rise again.
You are my anchor, my joy, and my reminder that I am never alone.

To My Colleagues and Friends

Thank you to those who stood by me during the aftermath of the incident —
who cried with me, checked on me, walked with me, and held space for me in ways I will never forget.
Your compassion in those early days made a difference that words cannot fully express.

To every friend who listened, encouraged, prayed, or simply sat with me during my recovery:
thank you.
Your presence carried me through a season when silence felt overwhelming.

To the Educators Who Inspired This Book

This book is for you —
the paraprofessionals, teaching assistants, teachers, counselors, school safety officers, administrators, and support staff who show up every day with courage and compassion.

Thank you for answering the call to serve our children.
Thank you for standing in the gap.
Thank you for being heroes whose names are rarely spoken, but whose impact is immeasurable.

Your resilience fuels this work.
Your sacrifices deserve to be honored.
Your stories deserve to be told.

To the Students Who Changed My Life

Every student I ever worked with, every student who trusted me, every student who walked into the ISS room with fear, frustration, or confusion —
you are the reason I served with purpose.

Thank you for allowing me to guide you, listen to you, advocate for you, and learn from you.
Your honesty, your struggles, your wins, and your growth shaped me more than you know.

To the Medical Teams and Professionals Who Helped Me Heal

Thank you to the doctors, nurses, specialists, and therapists who treated my injuries and supported my recovery.
Your skill, patience, and commitment restored what the incident tried to take away.

To Those Who Encouraged This Book Into Existence

To everyone who said, "You need to write this,"
everyone who reminded me that my story mattered,
everyone who believed this testimony could help others — thank you.

Your words watered the seed that became this book.

To Every Reader of This Book

Thank you for opening these pages.
Thank you for walking with me through this story.
Thank you for being willing to reflect, to feel, to heal, and to grow.

If this book inspired you, strengthened you, affirmed you, or reminded you of your own calling,
then the mission has been fulfilled.

You are part of this legacy.

To the KTURN Community

Thank you for embracing the movement of motivation, inspiration, encouragement, and empowerment.
This brand exists because there are people like you who believe in hope, growth, and purpose.
Thank you for walking with me as we uplift communities one voice, one book, one message, and one life at a time.

—

With humility and gratitude, thank you.

Your support, your presence, and your belief helped me rise — and helped bring this book into the world.

ABOUT THE AUTHOR

Ethan L. Ketterer

Ethan L. Ketterer is a writer, speaker, educator, and the visionary founder behind the KTURN brand — a movement dedicated to motivation, inspiration, encouragement, and empowerment. With a heart for service and a passion for uplifting others, Ethan has spent his life pouring into students, educators, families, and communities with compassion, clarity, and purpose.

For years, Ethan served faithfully in education as a paraprofessional, teaching assistant, and In-School Suspension coordinator. Known for his calm presence, his ability to guide students through emotional challenges, and his unwavering commitment to protecting student dignity, Ethan became a trusted figure in the lives of countless young people. His work extended beyond supervision — he became an advocate, a mentor, a safe space, and a steady anchor for students in crisis.

Everything changed on September 19, 2018, when an unexpected act of school violence forever altered the trajectory of his life. The incident left lasting physical and emotional injuries, but it also awakened a deeper calling within him — a calling to speak, to write, and to use his story to strengthen the very people who dedicate their lives to serving others.

From that painful season emerged a renewed purpose. Ethan transformed trauma into testimony, resilience into leadership, and grief into growth. His voice became a lifeline for paraprofessionals, educators, administrators, school safety officers, and support staff whose sacrifices often go unseen.

About the Author

Through KTURN, Ethan now creates books, journals, devotionals, and digital resources that inspire readers to rise above adversity, rediscover purpose, and walk confidently in their calling. His work reflects a message of hope, restoration, and transformation — reminding people everywhere that no painful moment has the power to cancel God's plan.

Ethan is a storyteller at heart, weaving his lived experiences into narratives that uplift and empower. His words carry weight because they come from truth, healing, and spiritual clarity. His mission is simple: to help others make a turn for the better — in their hearts, their homes, their work, and their destiny.

When he is not writing or pouring into the KTURN movement, Ethan continues to support educators, inspire leaders, and strengthen communities through speaking engagements, mentorship, and creative projects.

He believes deeply that purpose is born in unlikely places — and that every person has a calling worth answering.